SEA ISLAND
SANCTUARY

Jean E. Holmes

REVIEW AND HERALD® PUBLISHING ASSOCIATION
WASHINGTON, DC 20039-0555
HAGERSTOWN, MD 21740

This book was
Edited by Raymond H. Woolsey
Cover design by Bill Kirstein
Cover illustration by Jonathan Knight
Inside art by Mary Bausman

Printed in U.S.A.

R&H Cataloging Service

Holmes, Jean Elizabeth, 1941-
    Sea island sanctuary.

    1. Natural history—South Carolina—Sea Islands.
I. Title.

            574.90975799

ISBN 0-8280-0436-6

**Dedicated
To My Daughter, Becky,
Who Lived This Story**

Contents

Map of Sanctuary Island...6

1. Sea Island Sanctuary 7

2. Alligator Pond...17

3. The Turtle Woman...30

4. The Ups and Downs of Kites.................................42

5. The Prize..55

6. The Tail of a Kite...66

7. Sneaker Sucker Swamp 83

8. A Sanctuary of Worship..98

9. Raccoon Rampage...106

10. Heat Wave!..115

11. A Sanctuary of Memories.....................................123

Chapter 1

Sea Island Sanctuary

A bitter, cold wind whipped the ocean's spray into fluffy white foam. The foam scurried along the beaches in little globs, and caught in the rocks of the sea walls and jetties. It was early March on the little sea island that lay off the coast of South Carolina. An unusual cold spell held the normally warm and sunny bit of land in its grip. Lowering skies threatened an icy rain, or possibly even snow. The windbitten fronds of the palmettos had a brittle sound, and the sea gulls had flown inland to seek shelter from the approaching storm.

Becky and Danielle made their way, beachcomber fashion, along the windswept sands. Their heads were down as they scanned the beach near their feet. Occasionally they would bend over and pick up a shell or a bit of flotsam that had washed in with the heavy surf. But their movements were not relaxed and leisurely today, for the wind bit at their faces and their hands were numb. They had to keep stopping to turn their backs to the wind and pull the hoods of their jackets closer around their faces.

This was definitely not what most people would consider a day for the beach! But the two 13-year-old girls were not like most people. They were nature enthusiasts and shell collectors. They considered cold weather and bitter winds a small price to pay. To an avid beachcomber, an approaching storm means an exciting harvest. The nylon net bag that they carried was already full to overflowing with their treasures. There were several large moon snail shells and sand dollars, a beautifully sculptured set of unfolded angel wings, at least a dozen soggy strands of whelk egg cases, and an eight- to nine-inch-long whelk shell, as well as a good assortment of other shells and small sea creatures. The girls were ecstatic with their finds, for this was only the first day of their two-week spring vacation on the island.

This was Becky's fifth year of vacationing on the little sea island. She had come with her parents during her spring breaks and again during the summer months. She had grown to know the island as she knew her own backyard. Its beaches, tidal marshes, mud flats, and piney woodlands had become both playground and schoolroom to her. The visits were happy and carefree times, dampered only by having no one her own age to share adventures with. Her parents had solved that problem for the past two years by inviting her friend Danielle to accompany them.

Danielle was a vivacious little blue-eyed blonde who shared Becky's love for nature. Danielle's family had moved to the Southeast from Pennsylvania some three years before. She and Becky quickly became close friends. Becky delighted in introducing her to the flora and fauna of her native southland.

They both attended the same little Seventh-day Adventist church school. Discovering each other's similar interests had been an easy matter, for there were only 17 children in the entire school. Actually, the 17 students and two teachers were more like a big family than a small school. Most of them attended church and Sabbath school together, were members of the same Pathfinder club, and enjoyed many a Saturday evening social event together.

The two girls even carried some of their home activities to the island with them, for it was a perfect spot to work on Pathfinder nature honors. This was precisely what they were doing on this cold day in early March. They had each completed the Shell Honor during their Companion class. Now they were trying to finish the Advanced Shell Honor on their own. It was difficult, but they enjoyed a challenge. If they could complete this honor, they would try another of the

advanced nature honors, for the island was a place of wonderful possibilities.

The little sea island, at the end of a chain of barrier islands, was designated as a state wildlife and bird sanctuary. Conservation laws protected the habitat, and development was limited. Becky's parents had rented one of the few houses on the island. The house was built up on stilts just beyond the dune line of the island's eastern shore. It was a comfortable three-bedroom home built of wood, stained a grayish-brown to blend with the sand dunes and beach grasses. Two long staircases led to the main floor and to an open deck that surrounded the house. The view from the ocean side of the deck was stunning, especially at sunrise!

Becky and Danielle began to think of the warm cozy house as they made their way along the beach. They were approaching the house and could see a thin wisp of smoke being blown in a long horizontal line from the top of the chimney. It was like a beckoning finger.

Becky looked longingly toward the house and turned pleading eyes on her friend. "Dani, look at that smoke coming from the chimney. Mom must have a nice roaring fire going, and I'd be willing to bet that there is a pot of hot chocolate on the stove, and blueberry muffins in the oven. Why, I can almost smell them from here! Let's say we hang up this shell collecting for a while and get warmed up?"

Dani could do no more than nod her agreement, for she was too numbed by the cold to talk. They turned their backs to the wind and headed for the little boardwalk that went over the dunes. They didn't even watch for the treacherous little sandspurs that were often blown up on the walkway. The girls had their sneakers and heavy socks on so the sandspurs didn't bother them now, but sandspurs have an unpleasant habit of traveling in a sneaker until they come to some carpeting. Then they nestle down in the carpet where they can't be seen, and lie in wait for unwary bare feet. The girls had quickly and painfully learned that the nasty little hitchhikers exact a price for treading on the ecology of their sand dunes.

Becky tugged open the large sliding glass door. A rush of warm air and the smell of blueberry muffins enveloped her like a cloud of mist, and she felt herself going limp. She and Dani both dropped their wet, sandy collecting bags onto the carpet by the door and stumbled toward the fireplace. They collapsed in a soggy heap on the warm carpet.

"Becky and Dani!" Mom was standing in the kitchen doorway with an oven mitt on each hand and a stern expression on her face. "You two know better than to drop wet bags on the carpet." (They had just broken a cardinal rule in the list of "Rules And Regulations When Living In A Rented House.")

"Oh, Mom!" wailed Becky. "I can't move an inch, honestly. I've turned into a human icicle. My feet are frozen, my hands are frozen, even my brain is frozen!"

Mom smiled and relented. "Well, Love, at least your mouth isn't frozen!"

Mom picked up the bags and took them into the laundry room. Then she headed back to the two "human icicles." They were still lying in a huddled mass but appeared to be, at the very least, breathing. She reached down and helped them pull off their jackets. Great globs of wet sand plopped onto the carpet and mom had to bite her tongue. Now she understood the wisdom of the owners in putting down brown carpeting.

"OK, girls, when you've thawed out a bit I'll bring you some hot chocolate and a blueberry muffin," she said.

"Make that two blueberry muffins, with butter," mumbled Becky.

Mom smiled and returned to the kitchen with a sigh of relief. It was obvious that there was no permanent brain damage!

The girls managed to get down the hot chocolate and blueberry muffins in record time, which did wonders in the thawing out process. They pulled off their wet, sandy sneakers and placed them on the hearth to dry. Then they reached for a little pile of shell and nature books that stood on a table near the fireplace. Dani got two cardboard boxes with sides that had been cut down to about an inch in height. The nylon net bags, still filled with their treasures from the sea, were placed on large metal cookie tins near the boxes. Becky assembled the necessary tools: a bowl of fresh water, a sharp pointed knife, a pair of tweezers, a magnifying glass, paper toweling, and a bottle of baby oil. She also set a bowl containing fresh water and bleach in the sink.

The 13-year-olds spent the next two hours deeply absorbed in the wonders of their catch. They were like the salvagers of a richly laden Spanish galleon discovered on the ocean floor. Each treasure was carefully washed, gently scraped clean of debris, dried, polished, and finally rubbed with oil to protect it and bring out its beauty.

The shells that still contained animals, sometimes a hermit crab, were placed in the bowl of water and bleach. This was the easiest way of getting the animal out without damaging the shell. The girls, being true naturalists, did not enjoy destroying these little creatures so delicately and wisely formed by the Creator, but they knew that they had already been doomed when the storm had washed them up onto the beach. Life is often harsh for little sea animals. Becky and Dani were also good ecologists, for they never destroyed anything needlessly and they never took more than a small sampling of live animals and plants from any particular area.

The last of these two rules had been brought forcefully home to them just the summer before. The northeastern end of the island held a special secret—at least, they had thought it was a secret. A wide, swiftly flowing estuary, its waters reciprocating (river current and tide moving outward, followed by the tide moving in), had laid down wide sandbars that extended a considerable distance out into the ocean on either side of its mouth. During high tide the sandbars produced breakers in two different locations. The first ones could be seen pounding over the sand bars several hundred feet out. Then, as the current traveled over the deep water to the west of the bar, another set of breakers formed near the beach.

During the low tide even a casual bather could discover the secret. The receding water left large shallow tidal pools to the west of the sandbars. These pools of generally warmer water were the breeding grounds for a vast colony of beautifully delicate sand dollars. The sand dollar, a first cousin of the starfish, is highly sought after by many shell collectors (even though its hard external skeleton is not a true shell).

The two girls had often visited the sand dollar beds. Despite their shell collecting rules, they had discovered a good way to find a large quantity of live sand dollars. They would float on their stomachs in the warm tidal pools and extend their arms downward so they could grope along the sandy bottom with their hands. They sifted sand through their fingers as they moved along. When they felt a hard object they would gently dig around it. Usually it was a sand dollar and they could lift it up undamaged. They could have pulled up buckets full within just an hour or two. Fortunately, their better sense and respect for all living things quickly put a stop to any thought of greedy collecting.

To their amazement and disgust, they soon learned that not everyone shared their sense of values. One day as they were walking up the beach toward the north end, they saw a small group of people moving slowly about in the tidal pools. The girls became alarmed as they came closer. These people were treading carelessly along the sandy bottom, prodding through the water and sand with long-handled metal rakes and shovels. They carried buckets with them, into which they dropped hapless sand dollars. Obviously, they were destroying many of the delicate creatures. When they cracked one they unceremoniously flung it away.

Becky threw politeness to the wind and shouted out to the wasteful collectors. "Hey, you people! Don't walk on the beds like that! Lie down on your stomachs and float. You're breaking more of those sand dollars than you're collecting!"

A young woman in pink shorts and a flower-print halter top either did not hear the anger in Becky's voice or chose to ignore it. "Don't worry about it, kid," she yelled back. "We're doing just fine, even with a little breakage." She pointed towards the beach.

Becky and Dani looked in the direction she had pointed and let out a gasp. There sat six large plastic buckets full to the brim with sand dollars! The young woman was wading toward the beach and gave the girls a friendly smile as she approached. "Not a bad haul for an hour's work, is it kids?" she said. "I picked up nearly a hundred all by myself. Just think what could be collected in a few days time!"

"But why?" asked Dani with an incredulous tone of voice. "What can you possibly do with all those sand dollars?"

"Oh," laughed the woman, "it's a little business my friend and I have on the side. He cleans them up and makes jewelry out of them. You know, pendants and earrings and the like. I'm a bit of an artist and I paint pictures of beach scenes, seagulls, and such on them. It's quite a little money-maker and the gift shops along the coast buy them like hotcakes."

Becky had a feeling that the woman expected her to be impressed. Both Becky and Dani had seen sand dollar jewelry in the stores and had thought it was very lovely. But somehow, seeing this end of its production was different. It made it seem more like mass slaughter than art!

"Look, kids," said the woman, cheerfully. "Maybe we can make a little business deal. If you would like to collect sand dollars for us, we'll give you 50 cents for every bucketful—no broken or chipped ones, of course. We especially want the little baby ones. They're harder to find, but they make lovely earrings."

A look of anger flashed over Becky's face. "We're not interested in that kind of business deal," she retorted.

The woman looked startled. "What's the matter? Don't you like to earn a little money? Or is 50 cents a bucket too cheap for you? What else could you find to do to make that kind of money in a forsaken place like this?"

Becky tried to control herself but her answer was curt. "We can find plenty to do and it doesn't consist of ruining what's good about this island."

"Listen," said Dani. "Maybe you didn't see the sign when you came over the bridge to this island. This is a state wildlife and bird sanctuary. That means it's against the law to kill, injure, or damage the wildlife. That includes those sand dollar beds."

"Hey, come on, kids. There are thousands of these little devils out there. They probably reproduce 10 times faster than we can hunt for them," answered the young woman. Her face was becoming flushed and her anger was obviously rising.

"Don't you even care about conservation?" asked Becky. "One summer of just the two of us taking out even six bucketfuls a day would do tremendous damage to these beds. Add a few more people doing the same thing, or one good hurricane, and these beds could be totally destroyed." Becky hesitated a moment and then added, with a sly smile toward Dani, "It might even destroy your jewelry business!"

Becky's last statement seemed to hit home. The woman rubbed her chin and looked down at the buckets. Then she walked over to the water's edge and called to her friends. "Hey, come on. Let's try a beach on the next island up. We've gotten enough from this spot."

Becky and Dani heaved a great sigh as the greedy sand dollar collectors climbed into their car and drove away. "Maybe we do have a summer job after all," said Becky reflectively.

"What on earth are you talking about?" asked Dani. "You don't really intend to collect sand dollars!"

"Of course not, silly," laughed Becky. "The kind of job I was thinking of doesn't involve earning money, but it should bring lots of satisfaction. We'll be self-appointed conservation officers."

"That does have good possibilities," agreed Dani.

Looking back on that incident now, the two young conservationists realized that they had learned a valuable lesson that day last summer. They had stuck to their decision, not only in their own collecting, but by spreading the word to other visitors to the island sanctuary. There were too few islands like this left in the world. They had been taught to reverence not only the Creator but also His creation.

"You know what?" said Becky as she finished off the last of her third blueberry muffin. "I have a feeling that God expects us to spread respect and love for His creation right along with spreading the gospel of His salvation."

"I think maybe it's a part of the same thing," added Dani.

Chapter 2

Alligator Pond

Sanctuary Island was not the real name for the little sea island, at least not according to the current maps. The girls had given it that name, just as they had named certain places on the island that had special significance to them. There was a quiet body of water in the inland woods that they had named Coon Tail Lagoon after finding the remains of a racoon's tail on its banks. Then there was Fiddler Crab Marsh, Egret Tree Hammock, Moon Snail Beach, and so on.

The real name for the island had actually changed at least three or four times in its history. The Indians, who had inhabited it before the coming of the White man, had given it a descriptive name in their own tongue. The early White settlers of the coastal area had named it in honor of one of their illustrious citizens. During the 1700s, roving pirates had used the island as a hiding place and lookout point from where they could watch the coastal sea-lanes for unsuspecting merchant ships. They, too, had their own special name for it. The 1800s found the island to be a refuge for runaway slaves from nearby cotton plantations. They had their own code name for the island.

Current map makers have their own troubles with the names for barrier sea islands. An especially bad hurricane season can significantly change the topography. This very island had been struck by a series of three violent storms some 25 years ago. Those storms had eroded and gouged new watercourses through the island, turning it into three islands rather than one. An attempt had been made to give different names to the two smaller pieces of land, but the local residents tended to ignore them and still spoke of the islands as one.

The two girls, having spent some time researching this rather confusing history, had felt it quite appropriate to do their own thing when it came to giving out names. So the island became known to them as "Sanctuary Island."

The name had real meaning for them. First, it was a sanctuary for wildlife. Second, it had become a "human sanctuary" to Becky and her parents, and eventually to Dani also. It was a place of refuge from the fast-paced world of work, school, traffic jams, telephones, clock-watching, and deadlines.

Their pace completely changed when they reached the island. Their lives became governed by more natural rhythms: the changing of tides, the rising and setting of the sun, the weather, or even the change of their own moods. The easy-going pace did wonders for refurbishing tired minds and bodies. The island was not only a refuge but also a tonic to them.

Finally, the very name "Sanctuary Island" fascinated them. They had spent two entire quarters of last year's Sabbath school class learning about the Biblical sanctuary system. The first quarter had been devoted to the Old Testament sanctuary. They spent weeks constructing, from cardboard boxes and balsa wood, large-scale models of the furnishings.

Then in the second quarter they delved into the doctrine of the heavenly sanctuary, the role of Christ as our High Priest, and even the investigative judgment. This part had not only fascinated them but had become very real and understandable. It was like fitting the last few pieces of a jigsaw puzzle together. The background picture of the Old Testament services was now made complete with the new insight they had gained of the heavenly sanctuary and the investigative judgment.

The primary, junior, and teen classes had put on an interesting vesper program at the end of the second quarter.

They set up their model sanctuary in the front of the church. They even had the courtyard and the two sanctuary compartments, divided by curtains made of white bedsheets with large angels painted in gold on them. Their mothers and Sabbath school teachers had made costumes for them. There was a high priest, played by one of the older teens, complete with appropriate robes. He wore a blue skirt with pomegranates (small brown plastic pears had been substituted) and bells on its lower border. The breastplate with its precious stones (made out of melted plastic), and the mitered headpiece completed the high priest's costume.

They even had little cardboard lambs whose feet were attached to rollers so they could be pulled along with a rope. The younger children had walked down the main aisle of the church with these "sacrificial offerings." The entire program had been a great success and had been an excellent object lesson of this unique but vital doctrine of the church.

The girls often thought back to that experience, for it had given new meaning to the word "sanctuary." But they were realistic when they decided to use it as a name for their favorite place. They knew that there were no "perfects" on earth, not even this island or, for that matter, the Old Testament earthly sanctuary. The island was certainly beautiful, and generally a safe haven for them, but there was also danger. Above all, they knew that no one walks through a wildlife area without caution.

The problem is, a place like Sanctuary Island has a way of relaxing one's caution. The carefree way of life that even a few days on the island tends to foster, can make one forget that this is still a place very much ruled by the ways and the laws of nature. Then an incident can suddenly occur that provides a rude awakening.

It was just such an incident—actually two separate but related incidents—that re-awakened Becky's caution. The first occurred during her first summer on the island. The second happened three years later, during Dani's first spring there. She, too, was to learn one of the harder lessons that nature has to teach. Both events occurred at the north end of the island, which, appropriately enough, has a harsher environment.

The north end, along the estuary shoreline, was considerably more rugged. A granite boulder seawall had been constructed there some years ago to protect against erosion and to protect the bridge that connects Sanctuary Island to the next island north. A pier had also been built out into the estuary, but this had been virtually destroyed by a hurricane. The only portions left were the original wooden pilings, standing like alert sentinels guarding the twisted and broken remnants of the pier's boardwalk. The same hurricane that had demolished the pier had broken down the seawall, tossing the granite boulders about like so many pebbles.

The wooden pilings were now a favorite perching spot for ungainly-looking brown pelicans. They sat and observed their domain of sky and surf like pompous lords. But when they took to the air their awkwardness completely disappeared. The pelican has a wingspan of some six and a half feet. He can glide and soar on the wind currents with startling gracefulness. When he spots a fish dinner swimming in the water below, he will dive-bomb straight down, beak first, a distance of some 30 feet. He literally nets his catch in his "gular pouch," which hangs below his long stiff upper bill.[1]

The broken seawall, with its granite boulders in tumbled confusion, provided a perfect habitat for small crabs, snails, sea roaches, and barnacles, as well as a host of other little creatures that live along the tidewater line. Many of the rocks had been sucked far out into the deeper waters, where they remained submerged even at low tide. Slippery moss-like sea plants grew on their surfaces, and jagged sharp oyster shells attached themselves in the cracks and crevices. This barrier of rocks and sharp shells was definitely not a safe place to walk or wade through.

Walking was safer, though not necessarily easy, along the banks above the seawall. Here the land and vegetation gradually changed. First came the gently rolling sand dunes with their protective cover of sea oats, broom sedge, and grasses, such as bitter panic grass and nut grass. This cover alone would make the dunes not only lovely to look at but easy to traverse. But nature has ways of protecting her own. Scattered like a prickly mesh beneath these gentler grasses are the real menaces of the dunes. Wild bamboo, with its trailing thorn-covered vines; prickly pear cactus, with its long needle-like stickers; stinging horse nettle; and sandspur, with its removable pointed burrs, provide excellent "No Trespassing" signs.

Just westward of the dunes are slightly higher mounds of land containing saw palmettos, which are a scrub-like palm, as well as other wind-blown shrubs such as bayberries and sea myrtles. These shrubs survive well in the salt-spray air, and their roots retain moisture even in the sandy soil. Here and there are the taller palmetto trees, slash pines, and live oaks. These shrubs and trees provide a protective barrier for the less salt-resistant vegetation that grows behind them.

Continuing to the west, beyond the shrub line, was a broad field of waving grasses that provided excellent browsing for the graceful white-tailed deer that were plentiful on the island. They spent most of the day sleeping and resting in the heavier woodlands. In the early mornings, evenings, and nights, whole herds of them could be seen grazing among the grasses.

Becky had discovered this lovely field on an early-morning hike during her first summer. She was just coming down a woodland path that led out into the field when she spotted the deer. There were more than 30, peacefully grazing. A buck with an impressive rack of antlers stood between her and the herd. He lifted and turned his head in a stately manner, for he had sensed her presence. Suddenly, alerted by the buck, the entire herd turned and fled to the northwest. Becky was amazed at their graceful and swift movements as they effortlessly bounded over the tall grasses. They raced up a high bluff to the west of the field and disappeared over its crest.

She decided to follow their route, for she knew that this bluff was the highest point on the island and she was sure that she would get an excellent view from the top. She pushed through the tall grasses for some 100 feet when she suddenly noticed that there was a small body of water just ahead of her. Upon reaching its bank, she found it to be a lovely pond of quiet water. A little meandering stream led into the pond from the southwest. Becky decided that this must be a small tributary to the creek that ran through the center of the island. It was the branching of that creek that created the three separate islands.

The pond was such a tranquil spot that she sank down onto the sand along the bank and just lay there, soaking up the warm early morning rays of the sun. Hardly a ripple disturbed the surface of the water. She picked up a small flat stone and skipped it over the surface. Gradually widening concentric circles spread out from each spot where the stone had touched. The circles intertwined and made a lovely water chain. Becky stared in fascination.

Suddenly something appeared in the center of one of the circles. It looked like two little knobs on the end of a log. Becky stood up to get a better view. With a start she realized that the log was stealthily moving toward her. She slowly backed up the bank. "An alligator!" exclaimed Becky out loud. "It's a humongous alligator!" "Humongous" was a favorite expression, along with "yuck" and "gross". She and her friends liked using those words, even if they were not appropriate. But, somehow, humongous seemed very appropriate for that alligator. Becky estimated him to be at least eight feet long, and he definitely had a hungry expression on his face!

She decided that it was time to continue her hike. "Let's see, what was I going to climb up that bluff for? Oh, yeah, deer. I was going to follow the deer." She headed through the field and followed the pointed, split-hoof tracks that the animals had left in the muddy soil near the base of the bluff.

Animal tracking was one of her favorite hobbies; she had

collected quite a few plaster casts of animal tracks that she had found. She could easily identify deer, racoon, possum, rabbit, squirrel, and otter tracks. She was hoping to get some casts of a bobcat or even the tiny tracks of a cotton rat here on the north end. She had her casting equipment along with her, in a little backpack.

She became so absorbed in her tracking that she did not notice the large black dog sitting on the top of the bluff watching her. The happy, panting grin on the dog's face and the wiggling of his hindquarters made it obvious that he knew and liked her. But evidently the scare she had had at the pond had somewhat unnerved her. When she suddenly looked up and saw the looming figure of a large black animal, she let out a scream, lost her balance, and began tumbling down the steep bluff. The dog bounded around her as she slid, happily barking his enjoyment of this new "game."

"Taco!" said Becky when she finally reached the bottom and recovered her breath. "You crazy dog! You nearly scared me to death—not to mention that I could have broken my neck!"

Taco licked her face with energetic delight. He was a young Doberman; he looked full grown but he was still wound tight with puppy energy. Becky's family and Taco's family had become friends when they first met a few weeks ago. His two adult owners, Mr. and Mrs. Howard, and his young master and mistress, nine-year-old twins, were one of the few other families that lived on the island.

Becky had been pleased when she first met the family. She thought it would be fun to have some kids her own age to play with, since she was also 9 years old at the time. Things hadn't turned out quite that way, however. The twins tended to be selfish with their toys, and they often spoke rudely, not only to their friends but also to their parents and to each other. Nor did they have the same appreciation and enthusiasm for the world of nature that Becky had.

On the very first weekend the twins, Jerry and Jennifer, let Becky know exactly were she stood. Their parents had invited Becky to come with their family to a parade that was being held in town on the mainland. The parade was scheduled for Saturday morning and they were going to pack a picnic lunch so they could stay for a band concert in the afternoon.

It sounded like lots of fun but Becky did not hesitate to tell them that she could not go. "Oh, don't worry, dear," said Mrs. Howard. "I'll talk with your folks. I'm sure they'll let you go."

"Oh, they would be glad to let me go on any other day," responded Becky. "It does sound like lots of fun. But, you see, I can't go on Saturday. Saturday is our Sabbath.

"What's a Sabbath?" interrupted Jennifer.

"It is our day of worship," said Becky. "We're Seventh-day Adventists. We go to Sabbath school and church on that day." Becky hesitated a moment. She wasn't sure how much of an explanation was needed. "Well, uh, we usually go to church on Saturday. But we haven't found any Adventist churches in the towns nearby yet. Right now we're holding our own services, just our family, at the house."

"Oh, yes, of course dear," said Mrs. Howard with a pleasant smile. "Certainly we understand. We'll keep our eyes open in our travels. Maybe we can help you find a church."

Becky smiled her appreciation at Mrs. Howard.

Jerry was staring at Becky in amazement. "You mean to tell me that you'd rather go to church than to a parade and band concert? Wow! What kind of a nerd are you, anyway?"

"Jerry!" gasped his mother. "What a terrible thing to say!" She turned quickly and gave Becky a pat on the head, adding with obvious embarrassment, "Please excuse Jerry. I don't know where his manners are, sometimes! We'll just make some plans to go someplace interesting on another day." She turned and gave Jerry a thunderous look but he just shrugged his shoulders and walked away.

Becky never felt comfortable around the twins after that, but her parents still socialized with their's so she was often forced to put up with their rude snubs and snide remarks. The only real enjoyment she got out of visiting their home was in the opportunities she had to play with their dog, Taco. Taco adored her, even though his young master and mistress did not.

Taco was plainly demonstrating that adoration now as he bounded around her there at the bottom of the bluff. He raced about in circles until he found a good size stick. Then he pounced up on Becky and literally begged her to throw it for him. This was his favorite game. Becky threw the stick with a quick, underhand thrust. Taco bounded after it with glee. When he reached the stick he turned and crouched down beyond it, keeping his hindquarters and stubby little cropped tail in the air. With a playful growl, which meant "Come and get me," he began to move backward, pulling the stick with him.

Becky tried to catch him, but Taco was certainly better at this game than she was. He ran about with complete abandon, tossing the stick with a flick of his head, then grasping it again. Becky noticed that his playful romping was taking him very close to the pond. She knew how much Taco liked to swim. She gave him a firm command to come to her.

But Taco was too far gone into the game. He raced to the edge of the pond and began splashing around in the shallow water, shaking the stick in mock attack. With a sudden flick of his head, the stick flew into the air, landing in deeper water. Taco swam after it in hot pursuit.

"Oh, no! Taco, come back!" yelled Becky. She ran toward the pond as fast as she could. She had already sighted the elevated eyes and sharp ridged back of the alligator moving slowly but steadily toward the unsuspecting dog.

She stood frozen on the bank watching what she felt surely would be the end of Taco. There was nothing she could do to save the dog—but she could pray. Her prayer was short and to the point: "Jesus, please help Taco!"

She had hardly gotten the last word out of her mouth when she heard a shrill whistle from the top of the bluff. Jerry! It was Jerry! The dog responded instantly to that familiar whistle. He swam quickly to the shore and began racing through the field toward his young master. Becky collapsed on the bank and breathed a heartfelt "Thank You, Lord!"

Jerry scolded her royally when he met her walking through the field toward him. "Are you crazy? Don't you know that there are alligators in these ponds? Do you want to get my dog killed or something?" Becky tried to explain but Jerry wouldn't listen. He shoved her roughly away from him. "Oh, go on home!" he shouted. Then he stomped off towards the woods, with Taco playfully nipping at his heels.

Becky tended to avoid the "Alligator Pond," as it was known to her from that point on. But she still enjoyed excursions to the north end, for its habitat was so varied from the rest of the island. Becky found it to be an exceptionally good collection area, especially just after a good "nor'easter."

It was just such a nor'easter, during Dani's first spring on the island, that led the girls to venture up along the rocky northern coastline to do some shelling and tracking. Dani was just learning the fine art of tracking, and she had become fascinated by some exceptionally large raccoon tracks. The storm's surge had evidently washed large amounts of sand and silt down the river into the estuary, and the strong undertow had deposited it in wide exposed sandbanks along the island's northeast tip.

The girls hiked along the eastern beach until they reached the northeast headland. They were amazed at the wide sandbanks that had been formed well into the mouth of the estuary. The sandbanks were scattered with debris from the storm. Becky immediately spotted the remains of several large horseshoe crabs. She had just been studying about this odd creature and was delighted to find some.

Becky had discovered that this large sea creature, with his brown hoof-like plate of armor, was not actually a real crab. And, despite the sizable outer shell, the living animal underneath the armor was not very large. Appearances can be quite deceptive in nature. The horseshoe crab is actually a saltwater scorpion, a member of the spider family. His shell may grow to measure some two feet in length, but the

creature inside is only a few inches long.[2]

While Becky investigated the horseshoe crabs, Dani decided to follow the raccoon tracks. The tracks stopped abruptly at the broken seawall, but Dani climbed to the top and was able to pick them up again in the soft mud. They led into the field. Here the tall grasses had been pushed to either side, and the smaller broken grasses and packed earth of the trail showed occasional tracks in the muddy spots. Smaller branching trails meandered off to either side, but Dani decided to follow the main trail. It led to a lovely little pond that had not been visible from the side of the field.

Dani skirted around its banks and was soon able to find more of the large raccoon tracks. She was quite pleased with herself. She had been able to track the animal a good distance, and now she discovered the reason for its direct route to the pond. There, in the shallow water, were numerous broken shells, the obvious remains of a raccoon's dinner.

She sat on the sandy bank and pulled off her sneakers and socks. The water was cold but refreshing to her tired feet. She began wading around, searching for some live specimens of the snails. She had not even noticed that an eight-foot alligator had been sunning himself on the opposite bank. Nor did she hear his approach, for it was noiseless. The alligator slipped smoothly into the water and submerged everything but his eyes, hardly causing a ripple in the water as he moved.

Dani had her back toward the center of the pond and was busily inspecting some snail eggs that she had found on the waving water reeds. She splashed about, happy in her discovery, oblivious to the danger lurking behind her. The alligator swam to the center of the pond, where he could size up his prey. Then, in what appeared to be slow motion, he stroked his tail in smooth but strong S-curves that propelled him forward, gradually bringing him closer to the unsuspecting child wading near the bank.

But Danielle was not to be the meal for an alligator today, for surely her guardian angel was watching over her. Suddenly, a great blue heron rose up from the reeds on the opposite side of the pond, his large wings beating the air as he pulled his long legs upward.

Startled by the sound, Dani turned to discover its cause. She first spotted the heron and was enthralled to see this great wading bird of the marshes so close at hand. But her pleasure turned to shock and then to terror when she spotted the huge reptile moving toward her. He was now so close that she could see his entire body length.

She let out a scream and scrambled for the sandy bank. In her blind panic she could make no progress through the loose sliding sand. Suddenly, a hand reached out and grasped her by the shoulder. She was being pulled upward. She looked up into a face that seemed to mirror her own terror. It was her friend Becky, panting from her mad dash through the field.

"I forgot, Dani! I forgot to tell you about the alligator pond!" Becky was pulling her friend away from the pond as she gasped out the words. "I knew there was a large 'gator in that pond, but I thought you were still on the beach with me. When I heard you scream, I knew right away where you were."

The girls headed back over the rocks to pick up the horseshoe crab. They spoke very little as they walked thoughtfully down the beach. But they were both thankful in their hearts, for they knew that they had a Heavenly Father watching over them—even when they unwittingly waded in alligator ponds!

---

[1] T. Ballantine, *Tideland Treasures,* Deerfield Publishing, Inc., 1983, p. 136.
[2] K. T. Gosner, *A Field Guide to the Atlantic Seashore,* Houghton, Mifflin Co., 1979, pp. 202, 203.

Chapter 3

The Turtle Woman

The mighty constellation Hercules strode across the night sky, chased by the full moon cresting the eastern horizon. To the south lay Scorpius, its long tail flicking the sea like a giant fishhook. The blazing stars of the summer sky were gradually fading, washed away by moonlight.

Lying on a beach still warm from the baking rays of the June sun, Becky tried to trace the patterns of the constellations. The Big Dipper with its arrow stars pointing to the North Star in its smaller counterpart; the patterns of Hercules and Scorpius—these were easy to identify. But Aquila the Eagle was nearly obliterated by the moon's luminous glow. Only conspicuous Altair, the brightest star of the constellation, could be clearly seen.

Her eyes moved down to the breaking waves of the constantly moving sea. The waters were reaching their highest crest, pulled by the gravitational force of the moon. The white foam of the breakers reflected its sheen and created a pathway of light that ended in the fringes of the tidal pools.

The sea held lights of its own, millions of flickering greenish-white star points. This phosphorescence, or "bioluminescence," is produced by minute one-celled animals called plankton. The phenomenon of living light is usually seen in the warm waters along southern coastlines. A chemical reaction within the bodies of the tiny plankton, similar to the chemistry of the firefly, produces this eerily beautiful light.[1]

Becky never tired of watching this spectacle of twinkling stars and flickering water lights, which looked like a vast display of miniature fireworks. It was almost hypnotizing, for if she watched it long enough she felt that she, too, was suspended in a fluid of light.

She shook herself loose from her reverie, for she felt the importance of this night. She had spent more than a week of such evenings, walking the beaches and watching. There was a very special sort of creature that she was watching for.

The creature that she sought was a massive sea turtle known as a loggerhead. The great ocean-going reptile can grow to a weight of more than 300 pounds; some as heavy as 600 to 700 pounds have been found. The length of its large reddish-brown upper shell, or carapace, measures some four feet across. The undershell, or plastron, is softer and yellow in color. Older loggerheads, who have spent many years traveling the lanes of their saltwater environment, are often so encrusted with barnacles and marine grasses that they look like a swimming version of an ancient coral reef.

The name loggerhead was given to this species of turtle in tribute to its massive head and neck. It tends to look like a log well-seasoned by its passage through seas, which have smoothed, molded, and gouged at will. The large horny beak projecting over a toothless mouth appears formidable and threatening, but, in fact, it is quite a docile creature and would not attack unless placed in a life-threatening situation. It has even been known to swim unharmed through sharks, though larger sharks and killer whales are its natural enemies.[2] The loggerhead usually chooses flight rather than fight, despite its strong armor and protective beak.

Becky began walking the moonlit beach. Occasionally she scanned the luminous waves in hopes of seeing the great reptile rise from them, like a prehistoric creature rising from the Flood, seeking the questionable safety of land to lay its eggs. Though the sea is its natural home, the warm southern beaches are its berthing place. Becky knew that the time was right. A warm early summer evening, a full moon, and spring flood tide are the haunting siren calls to the loggerhead mother.

Becky thought she saw a dark form breaking through the waves, and she concentrated her full attention on the spot. Could it be? Yes—*yes!* It was moving toward the beach, flapping its flippered forelegs like a great bird, forced from its natural environment to enter an alien world.

Becky was so intent and enthralled by the drama before her that she sensed rather than heard a woman approaching from the dune line. The woman quietly stood by the child, each one only slightly aware of the other's presence. They stood as though enchanted.

The woman whispered, "She has come to lay her eggs!" And the child, without surprise at the woman's sudden appearance from the night, returned the simple answer, "Yes, I've been watching for her."

It all seemed so right, their being here together, as the great loggerhead made her agonizingly slow and difficult passage up through the sand for her appointed time. The young girl, a lover of the world of nature, and the woman, a protector of a small but vital part of that world, stood together to watch this wondrous miracle ordained by nature's God.

Becky had known this woman for several weeks, drawn to her by their mutual interest in learning the secrets of nature. The woman lived on the island, near the southern shore. She and her husband had come here to retire. She had indeed found a rest from the labor for money, replacing it with a labor of love. Here she had found a purpose and a cause and had soon gained the respected title of "the Turtle Woman."

The cause of conservation meets one of its greatest challenges in the protection of endangered species, and the sea turtles are fast becoming a prominent member of that unfortunate vanishing company. Their ocean environment is not the underlying cause of this precarious position; rather, it is their need to rise from the ocean to lay their fragile, egg-encased offspring in nests of sand that places their survival in jeopardy.

The sandy world of the beach is full of enemies. The danger begins when the eggs are first laid in the nest. It continues throughout the one- to two-months incubation period. Once hatched, the young must defy a host of hungry enemies to reach the sea. It is a perilous journey that only a few will survive.

Nest marauders—the raccoon being the most prominent of these, and ghost crabs coming in a close second—can demolish every one of the 100 to 125 eggs in a nest while it is still only hours old.[3] The baby turtles that hatch from the nest and begin their trek to the ocean face even greater dangers. Seagulls and other shorebirds take a fearful toll of the hatchlings. Or their way may be blocked by structural changes to the beach. This is where man becomes the greatest of enemies. Beachfront construction destroys not only numerous turtle nests each year but also mile upon mile of nesting areas.

But all is not yet lost for the loggerhead sea turtle. There are concerned states, South Carolina being one of them, that have passed laws and instituted programs to protect these wonderful treasures of nature. This is where the Turtle Woman found her place in the important work of conservation.

She had come from a small midwestern town and, until her arrival on the island sanctuary, she had known very little of the ocean or its creatures. It was a wonderful world to her. Beachcombing became her favorite pastime, and she spent many hours roaming the sandy boundaries of her new home.

One day, while making her way along the beach toward the north end of the island, she spotted a large object in the surf some distance ahead of her. At first, it looked like a boulder with waving brown seaweed. But as she approached it, she realized that the wave action was washing it toward the beach. No boulders that she knew of could be moved that easily by waves as gentle as those on this summer day.

A sad sight met her eyes when she got close enough to make out the object. It was the decaying remains of a full-grown loggerhead turtle. The waving brown substance that she thought was seaweed was, in fact, the shredded remnants of a net. The great reptile's carapace and flippers were still entangled in the torn netting. What a sad end for such a gentle and noble creature! More than likely, it had become so entangled, even after tearing from the main net, that it had not been able to surface in order to breath. It had literally drowned!

The woman realized that no conservation laws could save the loggerheads from shrimp and fish nets. Shrimping was a major industry along this coastal area. Unfortunately, the shrimp makes up a large portion of the loggerheads' diet, too. But while the shrimper may consider the great turtle a menace to his nets, the creature is really no match for man's efforts to reap the sea. The woman realized that a sight such as this was not altogether uncommon where shrimping is a way of life.

She wondered about this great turtle. Could it have been a female come to these shores to lay her eggs as she had done in years past? The woman started to pull away the netting so that she could examine the loggerhead in more detail. Then she saw the metal tag clipped onto one of the front flippers. Her heart seemed to skip a beat when she read the tag. It had been placed there by the South Carolina Department of Conservation just two years before. The date and the place where the turtle had been caught and tagged were plainly marked. It had been here, on this very island!

The woman tried to move the turtle further up onto the beach, but despite all her tugging she could not budge it. Would the tide wash the creature out before she could get help? She would simply have to take the chance. She started back down the beach toward her home, anxious to call the Conservation Department offices in Charleston as quickly as possible.

She had reached the little dirt road that led to her home

when she saw a child on a bicycle. It was Becky, coming down to the south end to do some exploring. The woman had never met Becky before, but she felt instinctively that she would be willing to help. She waved and beckoned with her hand.

"Hi! I'm Mrs. Morten," said the woman as Becky approached. "I was just on my way to the house to make an important phone call. Would you be willing to help me out with a very special problem?"

Becky felt a bit shy at first, but she soon forgot herself when she heard of the discovery of a tagged loggerhead turtle. This sort of thing was right up Becky's alley! Would she be willing to go round up some people to help move the turtle further up onto the beach? She surely would!

Becky dashed off on her bicycle to begin her search. How many people would it take to move a turtle that probably weighed all of 300 pounds? Two men could do it easily, but where would she find two men at this time of the day? Her father wasn't on the island. He was unable to stay as many weeks as the rest of the family, for he had business to take care of.

Then she saw Jerry and Jennifer coming down the road on their bikes. *Humpf,* Becky thought. *They're the last people I would ask to help!* But there really weren't many people on the island and she needed to find someone fast. She hesitated for a few moments, arguing with herself. "Yes," she said aloud, "three kids and an older woman could probably move that turtle."

She swallowed her pride and called out to the twins as they approached. Her explanation of the project was brief. It was sufficient, however. The twins' eyes lit up; this sounded like lots of fun. Jerry especially wanted to see a 300-pound partially decayed turtle. *He would!* thought Becky to herself. They headed back down the road toward Mrs. Morten's house as quickly as bikes can go over sandy roads. Jerry, as usual, was showing off by skidding his bike from side to side, delighting in the 45-degree list his bike made on the turns.

Mrs. Morten was moving briskly down her back steps when

they arrived. She was over 70 but she moved with the quick and knowing grace of a 30-year-old. Her hair was the color of snow that had been sprinkled with cinders, but the face beneath it held an intensity of purpose and her eyes sparkled with anticipation. Even the wrinkles on her forehead and the lines about her eyes gave one the impression of an explorer searching the horizon for undiscovered worlds. A person always had the feeling that he should be running to keep up with her.

The woman recognized the twins immediately. Very little escaped her close scrutiny on this small sea island. Her first reaction at seeing Jerry was concern, though she did not show it on her face. She had learned, through the wisdom of years, to keep her judgment of character to herself. Young and middle-aged adults usually prided themselves on their ability to judge people on the first or second meeting. Mrs. Morten had gone beyond that. She now realized how often she had been mistaken. But still, there were things in this young boy standing eagerly before her that would need watching. He had possibilities; they just needed direction.

Mrs. Morten knew that Jerry had little respect for the wild creatures of the island. Wasn't it Jerry that she had caught digging up sea turtle nests? She had also seen him roaming the woods with a BB gun several years ago. She had reminded him that this island was a wildlife sanctuary. Jerry had casually shrugged it off. "I ain't shootin' at nothin' but trees." She hadn't really accused him, just warned him. There had been no hard feelings.

This turtle, she thought to herself, *is a different matter. After all, it's dead. Maybe getting Jerry to help out on this project will be beneficial.* She ran it through her mind as she started down the beach with the three children trotting along beside her. *Yes,* she decided. *Jerry will be my next project. I will do my best to teach him respect and appreciation for nature.* Her sharp eyes took on an extra little sparkle and she gave the boy a quick wink. Jerry responded with a tentative smile and then a beguiling grin.

The Turtle Woman talked with animation to the three children as they walked briskly along toward the resting place of the unfortunate loggerhead turtle. She told them of the wonders of the great reptile's travels through the oceans of the world. She explained how the mother turtles return to the same hatching grounds, and how they meticulously build their sandy nests. They listened with growing awe to the story of the tiny hatchlings making their way along a perilous beach to reach a turbulent ocean filled with more creatures ready to devour them. Then came the great mystery. Where did they go to do their growing? No one knew for sure. But scientists were trying to track their wanderings. She told the children of the studies that had been done on this very island, of the marking of nests and the tagging of turtles. And now, wonder of wonders, they were about to see one of those tagged turtles who had sacrificed her very life in a desperate effort to return to the hatching grounds.

Now Jerry's eyes began to take on a sparkle, too. That tag that the woman had found on the right front flipper was intriguing. But, unknowingly, Mrs. Morten had hit upon something that Jerry truly appreciated. She had mentioned that there was often a reward given to anyone who found and reported a tagged turtle.

Mrs. Morten's phone call to the Department of Conservation to report the finding of the tagged turtle had been well worth while. The authorities were delighted to hear of her find, for they were involved in an important research project. They wanted to inspect the remains of this turtle. Two young men would be coming down in a pick-up truck later in the day. They hoped to take the turtle back with them.

"Are they going to bring the reward with them?" asked Jerry. He could already feel the crisply folded bills in his pocket. "How much is it going to be? If we help you move this turtle, do we get part of the money?" Jerry was all business.

"Well, young man," answered Mrs. Morten with a controlled smile on her face, "I am sorry to tell you that I never even asked them about a reward. Furthermore, if they offer one, I shall quickly tell them to put the money right back into their research fund. Does that change your mind about helping us with the turtle?"

Jerry was crestfallen but his sister quickly jumped into the sudden silence. "Oh, don't pay any attention to him. We both want to see that turtle. I've never seen a big sea turtle before." Her eyes grew large and luminous with anticipation.

Becky watched Jennifer out of the corner of her eye. Maybe she should get to know this girl better. She certainly seemed to have more depth than her brother. She looked back at Jerry, who was now sullenly trailing behind. "Hey, Jerry, you old sea slug! I'll race you down the beach to the turtle. Of course, I wouldn't want to exhaust you. Maybe you should just watch from the side lines. Are you ready, Jenny?"

The sparkle in Jerry's eyes was rekindled by the challenge. "Oh, yeah! By the time you two get there that turtle will have decayed to shell and bones!"

The three children took off in a cloud of flying sand. Jenny was the first to reach the turtle, her small wiry frame literally gliding along the beach. Becky and Jerry came in at a photo-finish second. Jerry made a valiant effort to break the tie by plunging forward in a flying dive toward the turtle. His face slid through the sand. He came to an abrupt halt with his nose pressed against the great turtle's horny beak.

At first Jerry could see nothing, for he had gotten sand in his eyes. He lay there trying to rub it out, his eyes watering from the irritation. Suddenly he sat very still, took a deep whiff of air, and let out a loud and disgusting "*Ugh!*" He pulled himself to his knees so quickly that a geyser of sand flew upward and showered back down into his hair. "This thing is *gross!* You don't really expect me to touch this, do you?"

Becky looked at Jennifer with a slow wry smile lifting the corners of her mouth. "Brave sort of fellow, isn't he!" They both laughed and yanked Jerry to his feet.

"Pull yourself together, old man. We wouldn't want you losing your breakfast right in front of the Turtle Woman!"

said Jennifer. Then she clasped her hand across her mouth and looked at the woman in embarrassment. She had not meant to be disrespectful. But the woman smiled broadly at her. She knew that the title was not an insult. It was one of respect and would always remain so. She accepted it with pride.

The two young men from the Conservation Department arrived at about four in the afternoon. They were amused by the little group that met them, three 9-year-old kids and a spunky little white-haired woman. They took some notes and measurements and began loading the turtle into the pickup truck, the three kids doing their bit in the process. It was no easy job, for the poor turtle's remains were rather on the slimy side. Jerry tried desperately to put on a macho front through the whole thing, but the white and pinched look around his mouth and nostrils gave him away. When the job was done, they all decided that a good dip in the surf was called for.

Before the young men drove away with the loggerhead, they sat on the beach and talked earnestly with Mrs. Morten. "Listen," said the young blond named Chad, "you're just the kind of person we're looking for. We need someone who lives right here on this island to help with this project. A person who walks these beaches nearly every day during the nesting months could watch for turtle tracks and nests. Then the nests could be staked for identification, and possibly even protected from marauders. As a matter of fact, if you were willing to come up to Charleston and take a little training course in turtle biology, you could even learn to move endangered nests and incubate turtle eggs from partially destroyed nests."

Mrs. Morten needed no time to think out her answer. Her whole face lit up. "I'm your person!" she announced. "After all, I will have to live up to my new title of 'Turtle Woman!' She turned and winked at the three children.

Becky quickly wanted to know if she could be an assistant. Not to be outdone, Jerry and Jennifer wanted to be helpers, too. And so, the Sanctuary Island Turtle Watch Committee was officially formed.

As it turned out, the twins tired of the job in a few weeks. But Mrs. Morten had won an important battle in her campaign of teaching Jerry some respect for nature. Becky remained a faithful assistant throughout the summer. She was to look back at it as one of the best summers she had ever spent.

And so it was that Mrs. Morten and Becky met on the beach that warm moonlit night to watch the mother loggerhead make her lumbersome trek through the dunes. They watched her dig the body pit where she could support her heavy shell and body while she dug out the smaller bottle-shaped nest for her eggs. Each grayish-white egg was about the size of a golf ball and had a leathery shell that would allow just enough air and moisture in to keep the little turtle embryo alive and growing.[4]

"Look," said Becky in hushed tones. "She's crying! The mother turtle is crying! Is she sad to have to leave her babies to hatch out alone?"

There was no mistaking the tears that bubbled out of the corners of Mother Loggerhead's eyes and formed little rivulets through the sand covering her face. The large tears glistened in the moonlight, and the woman and child moved closer together.

"No, I don't think it's sadness that makes her cry," said the Turtle Woman as she put her arm around Becky's shoulders. "God has given her those tears as a protection. You see, she spends all her time in the salty ocean, except for the short periods when she comes ashore to lay her eggs. The tears wash the salts from her body and, at the same time, cleanse her eyes of sand. They allow her eyes, adjusted to an underwater world, to see better when she is on land. The Lord has wonderful ways to protect His creatures, doesn't He?"

"Yes," answered Becky, "and maybe He wants us to be like the tears. Do you know what I mean? He wants us to be another special protection for the turtle."

"I think you are quite right," said the Turtle Woman.

They watched the mother fill in the egg cavity. She used her hind flippers as scoops to pull back the sand. Every once in a while she would turn, rest her heavy body, then begin the process again. Her weight and the softer undershell would firmly pack the sand onto the egg cavity. When the filling-in process was complete, she used her front flippers to spread loose sand over the entire area. This was another protective device—a means of camouflage. Only then did she begin her slow and difficult trek back down to the waiting sea.

The young child and the white-haired woman stood silently on the dunes. There was nothing left to say. They had just watched one of the wonders of nature. The mother loggerhead had left the protection of her nest in good hands.

[1] T. Ballantine, *Tideland Treasures,* Deerfield Publishing, Inc., 1983, p. 10.

[2] E. R. Ricciuti, *The Beachwalker's Guide,* Doubleday/Dolphin, 1982, p. 50.

[3] J. Denton Scott, *Loggerhead Turtle,* G. P. Putnam's Sons, N.Y., 1974, p. 27.

[4] *Ibid.*, p. 22.

Chapter 4

The Ups and Downs of Kites

Becky's first spring on the island was a time of pure delight for her. Her own home was far to the south, in the southern tip of Florida, where spring is simply a lighter shade of summer. The reawakening of the earth here in South Carolina, after the icy grip of winter, was a new experience to her. She had watched the first tentative blooms of crocuses, jonquils, and daffodils with reverent awe, for it was like watching the process of birth.

Then the robins arrived, and Becky welcomed them as old friends. Robins had always meant winter to Becky, because they spend their winters in southern Florida, feeding on things such as the little red berries of the Brazilian pepper, which grow in wild profusion, ripening around Christmas time and giving a festive air to the landscape. She had watched the robins gather in great flocks, preparing for their northern migration.

One February her yard had been covered with hundreds of feeding, chirping, and fluttering robins. Becky was certain that there couldn't be a bug or worm left anywhere in that yard by the time they were finished feeding. That evening Becky and her mom had stood in the yard looking up into the sky, gazing in amazement at the thousands upon thousands of robins filling the air. There were great clouds of them flying north, fast and high. Even as they watched, the very tops of the trees in their yard seemed to lift off as their own special flock of robins joined the thousands in the sky. Long after the last golden rays of sun had disappeared, they could hear the constant chorus of chirping robins, turning the skyways into paths of sound. Yes, robins were old and treasured friends and it was such fun meeting them again in a portion of their spring and summer habitat.

But the science and art of flight is not confined to the world of nature alone. Air currents are capable of supporting even inanimate objects, such as airplanes, balloons, and kites. it was the last of these three that Becky discovered during that first spring on the island. Her dad had bought a simple but pretty kite for her, and the two of them had a great time flying it out on the beach in front of the house. There are few places that are better for flying a kite than an open beach, where the almost constant ocean breeze can keep a kite flying for hours. Becky had proved this many times on the beach in front of their rented house.

One of her favorite pastimes was to get her kite flying high and then anchor the spool of line by wedging it between the rocks of the seawall that separated the main beach from a smaller beach area directly in front of the house. The kite sometimes stayed aloft all day long, coming down only when Becky reeled it in at night.

This enclosed and protected beach area was a favorite spot for all kinds of fun. It filled with water only when there was an exceptionally high tide. Then the waves would come crashing over the seawall, sending geysers of water and spray high into the air. When the tide receded beyond the seawall, all sorts of interesting things would be left behind. Starfish and sea anemones, skate and whelk egg cases, and odd-shaped rubbery colonies of sea porks were left in the quiet tidal pools. Even in early spring, when the ocean water was too cold for wading, the tidal pools left in this area would quickly warm under the spring sun and provide for cozy wading.

The sand in this protected beach area would remain

water-soaked for many hours after the tidal pools themselves had disappeared. Then the area would be difficult but fun to walk in, for one's feet sank in as though one were walking in soft snow. Holes could be dug that would fill with water. The wet sticky sand was also great for building castles.

When this beach area was perfectly dry and firm, it turned into a super arena for kite flying. The first few years, when Becky was alone on the island, she would spend hours flying and doing tricks with her kite. Then in the last two years, when Dani was with her, they would have competitions to see which kite would go the highest or stay up the longest.

Of course, all of this activity was made even more exciting by the use of fancier kites. They had tried making their own kites but had never been very successful. They wanted colorful, odd-shaped kites, something that would catch both the eye and the imagination.

Becky's mom helped them take care of this aspect of the activity one day in early March. She drove them into the nearest large town, a trip of some 30 miles each way. There they found a toy store that seemed to have a special track into the magical world of childhood. The elderly couple that owned the store really knew about kids and kites. They had all kinds of kites! Some kites had long, multicolored ribbon tails. Some were in the shape of birds, ships, planes, or dragons. There were series kites with eight to ten different little colored kites on the same string. The list seemed endless. It took the two girls a long time to make a decision.

Becky chose a lovely diamond-shaped kite. Its color was royal blue and on its face was a rainbow that ended in a large red heart. The tail had six wide silver ribbons that fluttered about and glistened in the sun. It had a long keel, the bottom of the diamond tapering gracefully downward and giving the entire kite a long, sleek appearance.

Dani chose a large square kite called an "Indian Fighter." It was bright yellow, like the sun at midday, with the shape of a large white bird in graceful flight sewn into its upper left-hand side. A long, single ribbon tail, bright red, hung from the bottom corner. It was the kind of kite that would certainly catch a person's eye as it sailed high into the blue sky above the island.

But, unless its only purpose is as a wall decoration, the proof of the pudding of a truly beautiful kite is in the way it flies. Becky and Dani could hardly contain themselves during the drive home. There was a good breeze blowing steadily from the southeast, with temperatures in the mid 70s. A perfect day for kite flying!

The car had barely pulled up to the house when the girls jumped out like a shot and raced for the beach, now dry and firm at low tide. They had to assemble the kites first, and attach the bridle and flying lines. The attachments for Becky's were fairly simple, and within five or ten minutes the blue diamond kite was tugging at the line like a live thing, pleading for the joy of freedom. It sailed higher and higher, going up straight and true, as though it had important business up above and did not have time for idle skipping about on the sandy beaches.

Dani, on the other hand, was having a rather frustrating time with her kite. She had put the main kite together quite quickly, but the bridle attachment was complicated and did not seem to balance properly. Dani knew how important it was to have this attachment right, so she redid the entire thing several times, carefully going over the assembly instructions and illustrations. Then the tail wouldn't hang properly. It kept twisting to one side. It, too, seemed to have a mind of its own, one that quite simply was not going to cooperate.

Becky noticed the struggle going on beside her and decided that it was time to lend a hand. Between the two of them, they managed to get the bridle attached and the tail hanging straight. Becky's kite remained aloft the entire time; the spool of the flying line was anchored firmly under a rock. The breeze was still blowing strongly, and Dani felt sure that her kite, like Becky's, would need nothing more for launching than to hold it up and let the wind catch it.

But this was not to be. The bright yellow kite was caught by the wind and momentarily pulled upward. Then it began to dance about erratically. Suddenly, with a great shudder that rippled all the way down to the bottom of its tail, the kite lunged sharply to the left and dived straight down, impaling the upper two or three inches of its keel into the sand. Dani stood looking at it in wonder for a few moments, her mouth agape.

"Not to worry," comforted Becky. "It's just a little change in wind direction. Let's try it again."

What followed was a repeat performance of the first sad showing. But the girls weren't going to give up easily. They tried another technique. One of them held the spool and the other walked a few yards up the dunes with the kite. At a given signal, the kite bearer was to lift it as high into the breeze as possible and the one with the spool was to give a good jerk. The plan sounded good, but it didn't work. Then they tried the running-start method. Dani raced down the beach as fast as the soft sand would allow, pulling the kite behind her. But the kite merely twisted around and around on the end of the string; it fell unceremoniously onto the ground when Dani stopped running.

Dani's spirits were beginning to fall as low as the kite. How could anything that looked so pretty be such a dismal and complete failure? They made a few more attempts to run with it, to launch it from high on the seawall, and even to redo all the rigging, but nothing helped. This kite was obviously of the wall decoration variety.

The girls had started disassembling Dani's kite when they heard a snickering laugh. They knew immediately who it was before they even saw him. There stood Jerry on the top of the dunes. They were not sure how long he had been watching, but it was obviously long enough for him to have seen the kite fiasco. He sauntered down towards them with a smug smile on his face.

"W-e-l-l, girls," said Jerry in his best Southern drawl. "I see you-all are havin' just all kinds of fun down he-ah!"

"As a matter of fact, we were until you came along," snapped Dani. She was in no mood for Jerry's ribbing.

"That kite sho' is perty!" continued Jerry, ignoring the sparks of fire in Dani's eyes. "It is t-o-o bad that you-all don't know the first thing about flyin' it."

"OK, smarty," retorted Becky. "If you're such an expert, let's see you fly it!"

"Now, I sho' wouldn't want to spoil yo' fun!" Jerry was still teasing but he was beginning to back away, knowing that it would be inadvisable to get too involved. He lay down on the dunes with his knees bent up and one leg crossed over the other, his hands clasped behind his head.

"The problem is," said Jerry, dropping his overdone accent and trying to look all knowing, "the kite is too square. That long tail is off balance and the bridle isn't positioned right. The whole thing is unbalanced and top heavy. You'll never get that kite up!" Jerry was all cheer and encouragement. "Now, if you want to see a good kite, I'll bring mine over. It's a real beaut! Tapered and nicely balanced. Why, it could outfly anything, I bet. It'll even outfly that sissy-looking rainbow thing you've got up there," he said as he pointed to Becky's kite, still flying straight and high.

"And just what is wrong with the way that kite is flying?" retorted Becky. "It looks like it's doing quite nicely, even without your brilliant assistance."

Jerry considered Becky's kite carefully. "Oh, it isn't bad for just sitting up there in one spot fluttering around in the breeze. But all those separate little tails wouldn't give it the kind of maneuverability you'd need if you really wanted action."

"What kind of action?" Becky asked. She was beginning to wonder if perhaps Jerry had something more than just plain bluff in him.

"Well, like in a kite battle. You know, when you try to position your kite so that you pull another kite down or disable it, like tearing off the other guy's tail or snapping the flying string, or maybe in a kite race when you have to get your kite to a certain point before everyone elses. The kite flyers might have to travel over rough terrain and they need a good kite that's easy to manage." Jerry was obviously warming up to his subject.

Becky sat on the warm sand and dug in her toes. She propped her elbows on her knees and rested her chin in her hands, for Jerry had set her to thinking. She stared at her lovely blue kite floating peacefully below the puffy white cumulus clouds. Jerry did sound like he knew what he was talking about. *Oh, well,* she thought to herself, *that kite is much too pretty to be in a kite battle.* She would never want to see it torn or broken.

But a kite race, now that sounded really interesting! The island would be a perfect place for something like that, for there was little private property and lots of unrestricted beachfront. Becky began to get a gleam in her eye. By this time, Dani had reeled in her kite and had been listening carefully to the conversation. She had that same little gleam in her eye.

"Hey, Jerry!" called Becky, for he had meandered over to Dani's kite and was carefully inspecting it. "Jerry, have you ever really been in a kite race? I mean a long one where you had to travel several miles?"

"Not a real long one," admitted Jerry. "Last year at school we had a one-mile kite race along a jogging trail in the park. It wasn't the greatest spot because there were too many trees. My kite got all tangled up in branches before I even got to the halfway point. But still it was lots of fun."

"How would you like to be in a real long one, you know, a race that took most of the day?" asked Becky.

"Hum," said Jerry quietly. He was beginning to get the same gleam in his eye. "But where would it be, and how would we get more kids into it? The only ones around here who would be interested in something like that would be you, Dani, Jenny, and me. That doesn't sound too thrilling."

"This island is a perfect place for a kite race," put in Dani. "Why just look at all that wide-open sky!"

"And," added Becky, "if we made the course interesting enough, we certainly wouldn't need more than the four of us. We don't want something that's hard to organize. We just want to have fun."

Jerry carried Dani's kite over to where the girls were sitting and hunched himself down next to them. All his bravado and sneering manner was gone and Becky began to feel an unexpected wave of friendliness toward him. He was trying his best to restring Dani's kite and adjust the balance. Perhaps Mom had been right, thought Becky. They had talked about the "Jerry situation" several times and Mom had suggested that, despite Jerry's lack of interest in nature and animals, he might have some really "good points," as she put it. She had suggested that Becky try to look for the good points in other people and not just the bad things.

Jerry held Dani's wayward kite up to the wind again. A sudden gust of wind snatched it upward, and for a few moments it hung suspended in the air. All three children held their breath. The kite hung there, gave a pathetic shudder, flipped over the flying line twice, and dive-bombed straight down to the beach.

"Well, there sure won't be any long kite races for this piece of junk," moaned Dani. "The only thing it would win a prize for is staying up in the air for the shortest period of time." She gave the kite an angry kick and plopped herself down onto the sand in disgust.

"Hey," said Jerry, "that's a good thought!"

"What's a good thought?" laughed Becky. "You want us to see who can have their kite fall in a miserable heap the fastest?"

"No, no," shouted Jerry in his excitement. "A prize! We need to have a really great prize for the winner of this long kite race we're planning!"

A slow smile crept over the girl's faces as they looked at each other. "First we have to get some decent kites to race with," said Becky. "That will take some investigation into possible financial resources." (The "resources" that she was thinking of consisted of the money in her mom's or dad's wallet, and their willingness to part with a bit more of it!) "But then, you're perfectly right. The next most important thing is to come up with a prize that's really worth racing a long distance for."

"Then we have to plan a course for the race," added Dani. "The kind of route that would be a real challenge and would take most of the day. That's what we need!"

"OK, guys. Let's get organized." Becky was thinking fast and her voice rose with excitement. Past animosities were forgotten as the three young conspirators began to plot their course of action. Becky and Dani would begin investigating the ways and means of possible financial resources that very evening around the supper table. Jerry was to go home and get his sister Jenny excited about the project. Then they would meet here in this same spot tomorrow morning at nine to report on progress and to make further plans.

It was a happy group that met on the beach the next morning, for they all had been successful in their appointed roles. Mom and Dad had come through and agreed to provide financial backing for the newly formed "Soaring Eagles." They had come up with the idea of working in teams to add a little more spice as well as a measure of protection in case something should go wrong. Little did they know at the time just how important this part of the plan would prove to be.

Jenny had quickly agreed to the race and was as enthusiastic as the other three. She and Jerry were to race as a team, but they had such a fight over what they should call themselves that Becky and Dani began to wonder if they could even agree to come to the race at the same time. Jenny's kite was in the shape of a large bird with red wings, and she insisted that they should be called the "Flying Red-Wings." Jerry's kite had the picture of a large blue fighter jet on it; he was equally insistent that they should be called the "Blue Phantoms."

"Hey, you two," shouted Becky above the din. "Why don't you let us settle this for you. Actually, I think, the best name for your team would be the "Fighting Siblings!"

"I've got to admit," laughed Dani, "that title has a realistic ring to it. Come on, people, why don't you compromise and call yourselves the 'Red-Winged Phantoms'; after all, Jerry, the background of your kite is red. If we don't get on with the rest of our plans we'll waste away the whole day on this foolishness."

"All right, all right," grumbled Jerry. "If that's OK with Jenny it's OK with me."

Jenny nodded her agreement and the four went on with the business of planning for the race. Jerry told them that his mom had to make the long drive into town that Wednesday to do some shopping, and she had agreed to take the four of them in and drop them off at the toy store that sold kites. Jerry even agreed to give them some of his "expert advice" in finding good racing kites. Then they would all go to an old-fashioned soda fountain that had good lunches and even better desserts. They would make a real outing of the day.

Finally, they set about the task of plotting a course for the race. It was to begin down at the southwestern tip of the island, just east of the mud flats. They decided to get one of their moms to drive them down there about nine in the morning, so they would have a fresh start. Becky cautioned them, however, that they would have to check out the tide tables first, as that end of the island was low and was often covered during the peak of high tide.

The course would then take them along the beachline of Porpoise Fin Inlet to the sandbars at the island's southeastern tip. Becky and Dani had named this area Starfish Beach, for at low tide they often found small starfish stranded on the sand.

Then they would head north up the beach, past the area where the dead loggerhead turtle had been found, and on to the beachfront by Becky and Dani's house. The distance from the starting point to the house was about five miles, and they estimated that it would take them two, or at the most, three hours to make that distance. They could walk that distance in a much shorter period of time, but this was different. They would be going over soft sand and some rough terrain. And they would be trying to control and move kites along, probably against the wind for a part of the distance.

There was to be an enforced half-hour rest and lunch break on the porch deck of the house, to be served (unknown to her as yet) by Becky's mom. Each team would be timed from the moment that they stepped onto the porch. Any time that they remained on the porch after the half-hour limit would be added to their final race time.

The last half of the course would definitely be the hardest, especially after they passed Sand Dollar Beach. This was at the northeast corner of the island. They would have to climb over or around the broken remnants of Pelican Pier and make their way up the rocky coast at the mouth of the estuary. If the tide was coming in or was still high, they would have to climb along the rocky broken seawall to Sawgrass Bluff. They would then have to climb the bluff, work their way down through the sharp sawgrass on the other side, cross the swampy area at the outlet of Marsh Rat Creek, and then make their way along the seawall till they reached the finish line, the estuary bridge.

They were not oblivious to the dangers along that broken seawall on the north end of the island. But all four of them had clambered over it so often that they felt reasonably safe. And, as extra insurance, they would arrange to have one of their mothers wait for them up on the bridge. They knew that they would be really tired by the time they reached the finish line, and it would be great to have a welcoming committee to meet them, preferably with a car handy to drive them back home.

The four youngsters had spent so much time planning the race that they were surprised when Jerry looked at his watch and announced that it was 1:00 p.m. and he was starving. As a matter of fact, they were all hungry. Jenny had a bright idea. "Hey, Becky and Dani, why don't you two come home with us for lunch. I'm sure Mom would love to have you. Then after lunch, we can write out the rules and regulations of the race and we'll all sign them. That way, everyone will have promised to follow the same rules and the race will be kept fair. Maybe we can even draw up a map of the route we plan to take."

The idea sounded great to Becky and Dani. They still held some flickering doubts about trusting Jerry. But if they all signed the rules it would be sort of like a contract. He wouldn't be able to turn around and say that he didn't understand something. "We might as well give the kid a chance to be honest," said Dani, under her breath. Becky heard her and gave her a sideways smile and a knowing wink.

"OK," said Becky. "Let me just run in and tell Mom where we're going."

Within five minutes the four would-be kite racers were heading north on the little dirt road toward Jerry and Jenny's house. Jerry, as usual, raced ahead with his special "dirt bike." It was low and had large-tread tires so he could maneuver well on loose gravel and sand. Then he would come racing back at breakneck speed, heading on a collision course straight at the girls. At the very last minute he would swerve away, leaving his victims in a startled heap in the road.

"Honestly!" said Dani. "I'm trying my best to like that creep, but he doesn't make it any easier!"

Jenny shrugged. "You just have to get used to it. Just imagine what I've had to put up with all of these years!"

"Well, I can't say that I envy you," retorted Becky. "Mom said that I should look for people's good points. I'm sure Jerry has a few, somewhere. He just does a good job of hiding them!"

Chapter 5

The Prize

The problem was what to have for a prize. Every other detail of the race had been carefully planned. Rules were written and signed. A course was chosen, and even a map of their route had been drawn. They were now piled into the back of Mrs. Howard's station wagon, on their way into town for the big day of kite buying. All four of the children had the same expressions on their faces—their lips pursed together and their brows creased with thought.

"Look, guys, we've got to come up with something," said Dani, the frustration evident in her voice. "This is no everyday, ordinary race. Surely we can come up with a prize that's worth going to all of this effort!"

"I've got it!" shouted Jerry with a mischievous grin on his face. "The winners get Jenny's new bike!"

Jenny's mouth dropped open and then she made a dive for her brother, buffeting him with one of the little pillows kept in the back of the station wagon. Jerry responded in kind, only his buffeting was considerably rougher. The fight might have ended in real injury if Mrs. Howard hadn't come to a screeching halt by the side of the road and threatened to do a little buffeting of her own. Things quieted down for a while, but Jenny looked daggers at her brother, who, in turn, stuck his tongue out at her.

"Really, children!" pleaded Mrs. Howard, trying to control her anger. "Why must you have a prize? Isn't the fun and competition of the race alone worth it all? You're ruining all the pleasure with this constant bickering!"

"Oh, Mom!" moaned Jenny. "You just don't understand. Why, this is the biggest thing that has happened on this island in years."

"I think you're exaggerating a bit, Jenny," retorted Mrs. Howard.

Silence reigned as the foursome resumed their thought. Becky stared out the window at the passing scenery. For once, she had forgotten to notice the beauty of this drive. Now it came back to her as she stared out the window.

The elevated highway passed over long stretches of waving golden marsh grasses and water courses that rippled and glistened in the sun during high tide. The ocean tides that surged back and forth in a constant rhythm were the heartbeat of the marshlands, even here, some 10 miles from the ocean itself. When the tide receded, all this would be mud flats, cut through with rivulets of brackish water. But even the mud flats have a strange beauty. They teem with life. If the tide is the heartbeat, then the mud flats are certainly the soul of the marshes. They carry the breath of life into the very existence of this low country.

The solid island of land that they crossed gradually became larger and more substantial as they approached the mainland. Great live oaks, their gnarled arms carrying masses of gently swaying Spanish moss, like tattered gray shrouds draped over ancient warriors, lent a touch of strength and permanence to the ever-changing marshlands.

The narrow highway ambled along, crossing one little island after another, wending its circuitous way slowly westward. Along the roadside, on the eastern stretch of the highway, one could see a sparse sprinkling of small wooden houses and little garden plots. Some homes were nothing more than dilapidated shacks that hadn't seen a coat of paint since they were built, if then. Others were whitewashed and looked neat in their simplicity. But, whether the house was in sad repair or well-cared for, each yard came well equipped with a flock of chickens. Some even boasted a tethered cow or a fat sow with pudgy little piglets.

The occasional stores along the eastern stretch were far more predictable. Whether wooden or concrete, they all seemed to look the same. Each sold a small selection of everything imaginable, from milk and bread to fishing gear and chicken feed. Each had two ancient gas pumps out front, but that did not necessarily mean that one could expect to buy gas there. Regular residents on the sea islands had learned to fill up their gas tanks on the mainland.

As they approached the mainland, the houses and stores became more frequent and took on a more prosperous look. Whitewashed wood gave way to well-painted frame structures. Solid-looking brick homes set well back from the road under a sheltering stand of tall pines were more evident. One might still see a little flock of chickens in the yard, but definitely no cow or pig. And the look-alike general stores gave way to proper little shopping centers and modern gas stations.

The road was wider now, and impressed itself on the landscape. It traveled over a series of old but serviceable swinging bridges that pivoted about their central supports like turnstiles. The bridges provided a gateway for the river that wound its way around the little islands and through the marshes. The fresh water carried down by the river gradually blended into the salty ocean waters carried in by the tides. An estuary is formed where these waters mix and are emptied back into the ocean. The brackish water, created by this mixing process, provides a habitat for many plants and animals that are unique to the area.

The roadway crossed the winding river many times, following it upwards towards the mainland. The Howard's station wagon reached the last bridge and the children could see the picturesque town spread along the riverbank. The end of the bridge separated the shopping district from the beginnings of the oldest residential areas. A straight line of brick stores, their backs to the river, marched southward. Scattered among the brick structures were old tabby buildings made of river clay and broken shell. These structures were jealously protected by the town's historical society. A lovely park had been built between the river and the stores, its entrance guarded by two Civil War-vintage cannons.

To the north of the bridge paraded a row of impressive-looking antebellum homes in a pompous line. Their long porticos and tall white pillars gave the town a picture-book look, like something out of a guidebook to the Southeastern United States. The entire town had as much southern flavor as cornbread, black-eyed peas, and grits.

The four children began to come to life as they approached the town. They could hardly wait to get to that toy store! It stood on a side street, an old home converted to a wonderful shop that drew children like a magnet. Mrs. Howard parked directly in front and the children piled out and rushed up the steps. Jerry and Jenny, by dint of much shoving and pushing, managed to be the first ones through the door.

"OK, kids, listen up," panted Mrs. Howard, having lost her breath trying to catch her offspring before they lost themselves in the world of toys. "I'm going to leave the car parked in front of this store while I walk down to the fabric shop. It's just four doors down. Come and find me if you need me. Otherwise, stay here until I get back."

Jerry flashed a grin at his mom. "We won't need you unless you happen to have a little extra cash floating around. You could give it to us now and save the trouble of an extra trip, of course."

"Jerry Howard," replied Mom sternly, "your dad gave both you and Jenny spending money last night. Just make sure you keep within your means." With that she swept out of the store and headed down the street for the fabric shop. Jerry knew that they would have plenty of time for browsing.

Becky and Dani were already in the kite department. A separate room was devoted entirely to the display of kites; entering it was like walking into the middle of a rainbow. Kites of all colors and descriptions hung from the ceiling or were draped jauntily along the walls, their long tails stretched out like a spectrum of light. All four children stood in a daze for several moments. It was hard to know where to begin.

Jenny broke their reverie with a sharp gasp. "Oh, my, just look at that!"

They followed her gaze and then stood as though transfixed. There in the far corner, hanging from the ceiling in splendid isolation, was the largest and most stunning kite they had ever seen. It was made of a strong nylon fabric, built to last. The background color was a lovely shade of turquoise blue. From the end of its keel hung a multiple tail of wide, brightly colored ribbons. The ribbons were artfully draped along the wall and looked like a brilliant display of the northern lights. A peacock strutted across the face of the kite, its tail feathers fanned out in an arrogant display of beauty. The children were speechless as they stared at the kite.

Becky finally got up the courage to walk over and reverently touch the display. She ran her fingertips along the tail ribbons and gave a little shudder, as though the colors had sent vibrations into her arm. Then she spotted the little price tag hanging from the bottom of the kite. She gingerly flipped it over and gasped as she read the figure written on the tag. "Sixty dollars! It costs 60 whole dollars!" she exclaimed aloud.

"I have a strange feeling that Mom would consider that over my means," moaned Jerry.

"Well, that certainly is an understatement," added Jenny as she, too, came to reverently touch the kite. "But can you just imagine what this kite would look like flying over our island!" She hesitated as they all huddled close and looked with longing. "It's a nice thought, but it's way over the means of all of us."

Dani, who had been holding back, suddenly startled them as she leaped up and clapped her hands. "This is it! This is really it! We've found the perfect prize!" she shouted with glee.

"Oh, boy, the kid has finally flipped off the deep end!" exclaimed Jerry in disgust. "Just which one of us, may I ask, is going to shell out 60 bucks?"

"All of us!" squealed Dani, her voice high with excitement. "That's the beauty of it. No one of us alone could afford that kite. But if you divide 60 by four you get 15, right? Now that brings it a bit more down to our level. Well, somebody say something. What do you think of it?"

Light began to dawn in the eyes of the other three. They could pool their resources and possibly afford the lovely kite.

"Hey, wait a minute," wailed Jerry skeptically. "There's one big drawback to that. The one who wins the race gets the kite and the rest of us lose our money."

"Humpf," snorted Becky. "What happened to all that confidence you were throwing around the beach the other day? Now you're already talking like a loser."

"Actually," spoke up Jenny, "as long as we're working in teams, two of us will be winners. That broadens the field a bit."

"Spoken like a true optimist." Becky patted Jenny on the back. "And I have an idea that may answer our problem. Dani and I will probably be coming back in future summers. My folks have been talking about buying some property in the area. We'll plan on holding an annual kite race. The winners get to keep the prize kite, in trust, for one year. Then, whoever wins the race the next summer keeps the kite for the rest of that year. Of course, it would have to be shared equally by the winners." Becky gave Jerry a stern look to be sure he understood her last statement.

"OK," said Dani, "that settles it. Now, let's check our finances. Can everybody contribute 15 dollars?"

Jerry shrugged his shoulders. "Jenny and I only have five bucks spending money each. Should we hit Mom for the rest, Jenny?"

"Fat chance!" answered Jenny. "You know Mom when she gets into a fabric store. She's probably well into the plastic by now."

"Plastic?" questioned Dani. "What does that mean?"

"Hey, kid, where have you been all these years?" laughed

Jerry. "Plastic, as in plastic money. You know, credit cards. Boy, does Dad love that! That means our chances of wheedling another 10 dollars apiece out of him will be just about nil." Jerry slumped down to the floor in utter dejection. "Oh, well, it was a nice idea while it lasted."

"Come on, Jerry," encouraged Becky. "Don't be such a fatalist. I don't know about Dani, but I'd be short, myself. After all, she and I still have to buy the kites to race with. Surely we can find some way to earn the money."

"That's a possibility," admitted Jerry. "But what if somebody else buys the kite before we get the money?"

"Jerry, you know what your problem is?" Dani was beginning to get truly annoyed at Jerry. "Your problem is that you have a great imagination but it's all negative. Surely you could come up with something positive if you tried hard enough!"

Jenny interrupted. "Well, I happen to have a positive imagination and I intend to put it to good use. The whole thing is simple. We just go to Mr. Becket and ask him if he'll put the kite in layaway for us. That's what Mom does if she doesn't use her plastic money. We ask him how much he wants down on the kite and how long we have to pay up the balance."

"Hold it." Jerry's playful humor was coming back. "I have a better idea, and it proves that I have a positive imagination. Let's get Mom to pay for the kite with her credit card. Then, these two [he jerked his thumb towards Becky and Dani] can pay us back as they earn the money. Of course, I believe the going rate of interest is about 12 percent."

The three girls looked at Jerry in disbelief and shook their heads in amazement. "You are positive, all right," said Becky. "Positively hopeless!"

The girls decided to ignore Jerry and put their plan into action. Jenny was appointed spokesperson, as she knew Mr. Becket and had come up with the layaway plan in the first place. She approached him with their request and found him to be very helpful. He asked them to put one-fourth down;

that would be only $15. Then, they could have two months to pay the remainder.

"Oh, a month would be fine, Mr. Becket," assured Jenny. "We want to have our kite race as soon as possible, before most of our summer vacation is gone."

The children watched with rising joy and excitement as Mr. Becket lifted the lovely kite from the wall and carefully folded up its long rainbow tail. He wrapped it in a neat package and wrote the names of all four children on the outside.

But Jerry still was not totally convinced. "That kite is awfully big and awfully expensive, Mr. Becket! What if it's too big to fly right? A kite that doesn't fly certainly isn't worth 60 dollars!"

"Oh, it flies very well indeed," answered Mr. Becket. "It might even lift a little fellow like you right up into the air with it. How good are you at flying?"

Mr. Becket chuckled and patted Jerry on the top of the head. "To be perfectly honest with you, I've flown this kite myself, just to check it out, mind you. But of course, I have the wherewithal to stay grounded." He laughed as he patted a rather rotund stomach that was even now escaping over the top of his belt in contented folds.

Jerry had not liked that term "little fellow" bit too well and he was beginning to realize that he might have met his match in Mr. Becket. He was ready to spar back with a few words of his own but he shut his mouth tightly when he noticed the threatening glares he was getting from the three girls. But he couldn't resist having the last word. "OK," he blustered, "but you better give us our money back if it doesn't fly right."

Mr. Becket winked at the girls and chucked Jerry under the chin. "You drive a hard bargain, young man. But, I'll tell you what. If this kite doesn't fly well for you, not only will I give you your money back but I'll personally drive out to that island of yours and give you a free kite-flying lesson."

Jerry looked somewhat perplexed. There was a zinger in that offer, but he decided that having the last word wasn't so important anymore. He suddenly remembered that he had wanted to look at some model cars.

Becky turned to Mr. Becket and a grin lighted her face. For an old man, this guy was pretty sharp! She decided that she really liked him and could completely trust him. "Mr. Becket, we're going to have a kite race and I need a kite that's lightweight, easy to fly, and yet has a lot of maneuverability. Uh, by the way, it can't be too expensive." Quite frankly, she was getting very worried about her money supply.

Dani also asked the toy store owner for his help. She was looking for something with similar qualities, including the inexpensive part. Her folks had given her spending money for this summer vacation adventure, but unfortunately, her eyes had been a bit larger than her purse during the early part of the trip.

Mr. Becket was a jovial sort of fellow who loved children. He knew them well and he had rightly assessed the situation of these two as they told him of their needs. He also had a feeling that he knew exactly the kind of kite that each girl would be happiest with.

He helped Becky find a kite that met her requirements, but one that would also give wings to her imagination. It was small and lightweight, though it was made from a fairly strong plastic-type material. It was in the shape of an elongated half circle; the tail, actually an extension of the kite body itself, was very long and tapered to a point. The kite face had a large dragon's head on it. The dragon's body extended into the tail, which rippled backward in a series of three colors, arranged alternately in horizontal zigzag patterns.

Dani had decided on something more conservative. She did not want to risk any more dismal failures. She chose a cloth kite in a well-tapered diamond shape. The kite itself was a light purple, devoid of pictures and decorations. The tail, perfectly balanced from the tip of the keel, was light yellow in color. Mr. Becket himself assembled her kite right there in the store and affixed the bridle and flying line for her. No, indeed, thought Dani, there would be no more errors.

She intended to win this race—with Becky's help, of course.

Mrs. Howard arrived just as the girls were paying for their kites. "Perfect timing, kids!" she said as she breezed through the door. She had obviously enjoyed herself in the fabric shop, for the back of the station wagon seemed to be overflowing with bags. Living on a little island as she did, Jerry and Jenny's mom needed some absorbing hobbies. Sewing and needlework were her favorites and over the years she had become quite an expert seamstress. Her recreation was actually turning into a money-making activity, for she had found women who wanted her to make things for them, and they paid well for her neat and artistic work.

It was a happy little group that trooped into the soda fountain shop that afternoon. The soda fountain was one of those special stores that had come straight out of the 1940s with little change. To enter it was like walking back in time. It held a fascination for tourists as well as for the local residents. The shop always did a brisk business.

Luckily, Mrs. Howard and the children found an empty table right away. They ordered thick juicy sandwiches, crisp home-made potato chips, and milk shakes that were so thick and creamy that they had to be eaten with a spoon. The noisy chatter that surrounded them did nothing to dampen their own excited conversation. The children were again deep in their plans for the big race and the prize kite. They all needed to come up with some money-making schemes.

Becky had an idea that she and Dani were going to share. They would go around to the few residents of the island and try to find odd jobs. They needed about $30 between them. As things turned out, they only needed to go to one house. The Turtle Woman was going to visit her grandchildren for two weeks. She told the girls that she would pay them $15 a week if they would take care of her two cats, do a little yard work, and watch the house and turtle nests. This would give them just the amount they needed.

Jerry and Jenny, on the other hand, were not particularly interested in doing odd jobs. "Too much work!" as Jerry put it. He had come up with an idea of his own, and grudgingly he had agreed to let Jenny help. He had decided to do some crabbing and perhaps even dig for clams and oysters. There was a little seafood restaurant two islands west of their island. It catered to folks who liked to drive down the scenic highway for a day's outing. Jerry was sure he could sell anything he caught to the owners. He could also try a few of the little general stores on the eastern end of the highway.

Becky and Dani wrinkled their noses at anyone actually eating such stuff—especially raw! Both of them were vegetarians and didn't eat meat, let alone what they knew to be real scavengers of the sea and marshes.

They had spent an afternoon watching some locals "go crabbing." A piece of waste meat, such as a chicken neck, was placed on the end of a large hook attached to a long string that was, in turn, wrapped around a stick. The baited hook was thrown out into the shallow water of the marsh and would lie there quietly until the crabber felt a nibble. He would quickly jerk the line and yank it in. If he had a crab on the hook, he would dump it into a bucket of brackish water.

It didn't always work, of course. Many of the crabs got away with the bait. The quick little crustaceans weren't the least bit fussy about what they ate. They would gobble down spoiled and decaying meat just as quickly as fresh meat. It was not uncommon for the bait being used by the crabbers to sit for hours in the hot Carolina sun. The thought of eating something that had just made a meal from decayed meat was downright repulsive to the two girls. They told Jerry as much, but he only laughed and called them sissies.

Nonetheless, it was a happy group that packed themselves back into the station wagon around kites, fabrics, and notions. The trip back down the chain of islands and through the marshes was considerably more enjoyable than that of the morning. There was neither silence nor argument, for each one felt the happy glow of accomplishment. And each of the four children was imagining himself or herself flying that lovely prize kite over beautiful Sanctuary Island.

Chapter 6

The Tail of a Kite

Jerry stuck out his foot and dug his heel into the sandy roadway. His dirt bike did a 90-degree turn and came to a screeching stop by the rented house at the end of the small beach road. He dropped the bike near one of the supporting pilings under the house and took the back steps two at a time. "What's taking you so long, slowpoke?" he shouted, leaning over the top rail.

Jenny had peddled as hard as she could, but her three-speed was no match for Jerry's adaptable bike. Nor did she have the reckless courage for flying at breakneck speed over loose sand and around turns that Jerry did. She carefully pressed the brakes on her handlebars and brought her bike to a sedate stop at the base of the steps. She decided to ignore her brother's taunts. Then she propped her bike against the stair railing and slowly ascended the steps.

"I could care less about racing you," she retorted when she got to the top step. "I'm not even sure that I want to be your partner for the kite race tomorrow. It would serve you right if you didn't have any partner at all!"

"The fact is, Miss Smarty, I don't need you for a partner! As a matter of fact, I'd have a better chance of winning that race if you weren't along," Jerry snapped back at her.

Becky's mom, awakened by the screeching of brakes and the arguing, opened the door to find the two siblings still at each other. She had slipped on a bathrobe and was rubbing sleep from her eyes. "Jerry and Jenny?" she asked, trying to clear her throat sufficiently in order to make herself heard over the din. "I really hate to interrupt this little family matter, but may I ask why are you standing at my backdoor step at 6:00 a.m., shouting at each other at the top of your lungs? What's wrong with staying at your own house to do it? Or better yet, why don't you go find a deserted beach. There certainly should be plenty of them available, especially at this time of the morning."

"Oh, wow, I'm sorry!" stammered Jenny. "Is it only six o'clock?"

"I believe that's what my clock said, although it's a bit hard to read it in the dark. The girls are still asleep. Is that what you're here for?"

Jerry jumped into the conversation. "Well, actually, we thought it might be a good idea to get an early start into town. We appreciate your taking us in there today to get the prize kite."

"Early start is hardly the word for it!" answered Becky's mom. "We'd beat Mr. Becket to his shop by at least an hour or two." She stopped long enough to yawn. "Oh well, I'm awake now. Have you two had any breakfast?"

"We had some—" started Jenny but Jerry jumped in front of her and started talking.

"We just shoved a few crackers in our mouths. Actually, we're starving, especially if you were planning on making those extra scrumptious pecan pancakes. I like mine with plenty of butter and syrup."

"Actually, Jerry, cooking pecan pancakes was not the first thing on my mind when I woke up this morning," said the sleepy woman. "However, I'll look and see if I have any pecans. If the commotion hasn't awakened the girls, maybe the smell of pancakes will."

The little group was assembling at Becky's house this morning because her mom had agreed to take them into town to get the large kite. Becky and Dani had collected their money two weeks ago, but Jerry and Jenny had had a bit more difficulty in earning theirs. They had found out that it took an awful lot of crabs, clams, and oysters to receive $30 in return. They had planned on holding the race on July 1, if the weather and winds were right. The first day of July was tomorrow and the weather was looking perfect. Jerry and Jenny had come right down to the wire in collecting their share of the prize kite money.

All four of the children had been flying kites like mad over the past month. They had gone to various sections of the race route, but one of the rules had been that they couldn't practice by traveling the entire route with their kites. That was to be done only on the day of the race. Becky and Dani were pleased with the practice performances of their kites, and they felt confident and ready. Jerry and Jenny also felt secure in the capabilities of their kites. It looked like it would be a close race.

The summer sun rose over a watery horizon on the morning of July 1, to be greeted by the four kite flyers standing on the deck of the beach house. They could not have chosen a better day for the race if they had been able to look into some sort of crystal ball. It was going to be warm, but there was a brisk ocean breeze directly from the southeast. That meant that their kites would be flying ahead of them and in the general direction that they would have to walk. Large white cumulus clouds were forming to the northeast, but they didn't appear to carry any rain.

The children would have to wait till nearly nine o'clock before starting, because of the high tide that would surely be covering much of the beachline to the south. They needed a fairly dry beach for hiking. The sand on the beaches on either end of the island was well mixed with mud and silt that was washed down from the rivers. The outgoing tide left a thick muck that was very difficult for walking, let alone hiking. A few hours of warm sun, however, would firm things up quite nicely.

All of the children wore sneakers. They planned on taking them off and tying them together so they could carry them in areas of soft sand. But anyone who has hiked along a beach for several miles knows how hard the terrain is on bare feet. Also, the north end of the island was far too rugged for bare feet. But the children had been running around barefoot so much that summer that the soles of their feet were tough enough for nearly anything.

They had a leisurely breakfast on the porch deck and spent the next few hours checking out their kites. Extra bridles and spools of flying line, gloves to protect their hands from the constant pull and rub of the string, water canteens, sunglasses, sunscreen lotion, and some munchies to give them energy, were all included in the lightweight backpacks that they would carry. They even carried a few bandages and other first-aid equipment, as well as small knives, in case of emergencies. The children felt sure that they had thought of everything.

At 8:30 a.m., they piled their kites and gear into the back of the van and climbed in around it. Becky's mom had agreed to take them down to the south beach. She would then return home and wait for their lunchtime arrival at the beach house. Jerry and Jenny's mom was to wait for them at the north-end bridge in the afternoon. The prize kite, fully assembled, was waiting at the twins' house. There was to be a special award dinner there in the evening, with both of their families, the Turtle Woman, and Mr. and Mrs. Becket from the toy store, in full attendance. It was to be a very full and exciting day!

As they had planned, the southern beachlines were just beginning to dry out sufficiently when they arrived. Becky's mom asked them to sit quietly for a few minutes while she gave them some last minute instructions and warnings. The partners were to stay together, no matter what! If any real emergencies occurred, the other team, if they were within range to know that there was trouble, were to discontinue the race immediately and go for help. There were to be no unfair actions or tricks played on the opposing team that might place them in danger.

Becky was not surprised in the least when her mom, at the end of the list of instructions, asked the children to stand in a circle with her and hold hands. She knew what was coming, for to her it was a common practice. But Jerry and Jenny were curious. What was this woman planning on doing? Surely they weren't going to play some silly game before they started the race.

Becky's mom smiled at the twins and asked them to close their eyes and bow their heads. She then began to pray. "Dear Father, thank you for this beautiful day and for this lovely island. Thank you for the fellowship and fun that these children are able to have together. Dear Lord, I pray that you will watch over these young folks as they travel along the beaches on their race today. May their guardian angels be with them and watch closely over them. Give these children the wisdom to avoid danger. Help them to be fair and honest in their competition, and always to think of the safety and happiness of their competitors. Bring them all safely to the finish line. And Father, help them to show good sportsmanship, no matter who wins. In Jesus' precious name, Amen."

Jerry and Jenny stood in stunned silence for several moments. They had never heard anyone really pray before! They had been to church once or twice and heard prayers read out of a book. But they had never heard anyone talk to God as though He were a kindly friend and protector, standing close by. A slow smile began to creep over Jerry's face, and it wasn't a mischievous or "making-fun-of" sort of smile. Jerry was impressed! He really liked it. Especially the part about the guardian angels. He decided that he would have to find out more about this. Maybe there was something to this religious stuff that Becky and Dani talked about!

The four children assembled their gear and put on their backpacks. They checked the rigging on their kites and held them up into the wind. The four kites took off for the sky in a blaze of color and flying ribbons. The wind jerked them tight against the restraining flying lines and the children realized that this was going to be a test of stamina for the kites as well as for the kite flyers. Becky's mom drew a straight line on the beach and had the four racers stand behind it. Tension was high for the children. This was it!

The countdown began—ten, nine, eight, seven, six, five,

four, three, two, one—blast off! The children sprinted forward at a run. Their kites twisted erratically in the breeze, for this was the only leg of the race where they would actually be pulling their kites against the wind. Dani and Becky slackened their pace. Running was causing too much strain on the lines and this was no time to lose a kite.

Jerry, on the other hand, was running for all he was worth, with Jenny several paces behind, trying to keep up with him. "Jerry," she called, "slow down, your kite's doing nosedives."

Jerry glanced over his shoulder and realized his mistake. He stood still and waited till his kite leveled off. "I guess you're right, kid. This race isn't going to be won by running the whole way. Oh well, we got a good lead on the 'Soaring Eagles', or whatever it is that they call themselves."

The racers continued moving southeast against the wind, nursing their kites along behind them. They passed the sea turtle nests and saw the Turtle Woman standing on her high patio deck, waving and cheering them on. Becky and Dani were closing the distance between themselves and the Red Bombers, as Jerry and Jenny had decided to call themselves. Starfish Beach and the wide sandbars of the southeastern tip of the island lay dead ahead. Once around that turn, the going would get easier for a while, as their kites would be pulled ahead and to the left of them. They were all making excellent time.

But a surprise met them at the island's corner. There had been quite a storm two days before, one of those summer squalls that seems to come out of nowhere, accompanied with gusts of strong wind and high waves. Becky remembered that the umbrella table had nearly blown off the patio deck that day. The effects of that storm could still be seen on this beach front. Piles of broken shells lay scattered along the sand, with higher concentrations filling the long grooves left by the bulldozing action of the waves. Their sharp, broken edges made walking treacherous.

But another and worse menace lay sprawled along the drying sand. Small, blue balloon-like creatures with stinging tentacles spread for surprisingly long distances around them, washed up by the storm. Becky and Dani were well familiar with these potentially dangerous jellyfish, called Portuguese man-of-war, for they were a common occurrence along the summer beaches of Florida. Finding them here along the Carolina beaches was not quite as common a sight. But a good storm, coming straight out of the tropics, can bring in quite an invasion of these painfully stinging creatures.

The children had started the race in bare feet. It was obvious that they would have to put on their sneakers to get through this more treacherous area. Now the pace grew slower, and the racers had to pay more attention to the ground than they did to their kites. The sun was also higher in the sky, and its hot rays beat down on the children.

Jerry and Jenny were still in the lead, though not by a big margin. Jerry could feel a trickle of sweat running down his spine and prickling along his forehead. Jenny had gotten her sneakers wet and they were rubbing the backs of her heels, for she hadn't taken the time to put on socks. To make things worse, the wind had picked up, and the kites were tugging strongly on the lines. It was hard on the arms and shoulders. If only they could just sit and rest for a few moments, or even just stand still and anchor the kites in the seawall to give their arms a rest!

Jenny looked back at the two girls and tugged Jerry's shirt. "Hey, Jer, look at Becky and Dani. I think we ought to do the same thing."

Jerry turned to look and saw that the two girls had indeed anchored their kites and taken off their sneakers. They were wading, knee deep in the surf. Then they started splashing their faces with the cool ocean water. "OK," said Jerry. "Why not!"

He and Jenny anchored their kites firmly and sat down to peel off their sneakers. Jenny was the first one into the water, wading out to the breakers, which were thin and flat in the hot summer weather. She was just splashing the salty water on her face when she was startled by a loud splash near her.

Jerry was not content with wading. He had made a running dive, going head first into the waves. He surfaced some 20 feet from his sister, spewing a fountain of water between the gap in his front teeth.

"Wow, does this feel great!" he shouted back to Jenny. "Come on in and join me, kid." He turned on his stomach and breaststroked out into deeper water.

Jenny was hesitant. She had learned a quick lesson from the wet sneakers rubbing on her heels. Jerry had dived in fully dressed in his blue jeans and shirt. He had taken time to take off only his shoes and socks. "Jerry," she called. "I don't think it's a smart idea to get our clothes all wet with sea-water. Besides, we have a race to win." She started to wade back to shore but Jerry turned over on his back and headed further out, doing a sharp-looking backstroke.

Becky and Dani, in the meantime, had cooled off and were refreshed. Wading back to shore, they poured some fresh water from their canteens and rinsed the salt and sand from their faces and arms. Then they collected their backpacks and kites and headed up the beach. They passed the spot where Jerry and Jenny had anchored their kites but they made no attempt to alert the twins to their presence. After all, they needed every advantage they could get. It had become all too apparent that the twins were quick, strong hikers. The girls had decided to try the old tortoise and hare strategy. They would conserve their strength during the first portion of the race by simply keeping up a steady pace and not trying to hold the lead. Then, near the end of the race, when the twins would probably be more fatigued, they would put on the steam and push hard and fast for the finish. But as long as the Red Bombers were going to goof off, they might as well put it to their own advantage.

The twins still hadn't noticed Becky and Dani forging ahead. Jerry was too occupied with the relaxed feeling of just floating on his back with his eyes closed and his body supported by the salt water. Jenny, on the other hand, had her eyes on something else in the water. She had glanced to the south, just beyond where the low waves were breaking, and she had seen something cutting through the surf. She squinted and shaded her eyes with her hands. Yes, it was several somethings—three, as a matter of fact. They were heading in a straight line north, toward Jerry, and they were moving fast.

Dorsal fins! The realization of what she had seen struck her like the blow of a fist. "Jerry! Jerry—get out of the water!" She shouted as she tried to plow through the waves toward him. "Jerry! Get out of the water fast—there are sharks coming!" She was in blind panic now. There was nothing in all her island living that she feared more than sharks.

Jerry heard her last words with a start. He pulled himself upright, treading water and looking southward. Then he saw them too, coming closer. He knew his chances of outswimming a shark were about 1,000 to one but he sure was going to try. He darted one quick look to the south again; at that very instant three large forms broke the surface and arced upward, then came plunging down into the water again.

Jerry stopped dead in the water. He turned piercing, angry eyes on his sister, who was still lunging through the water toward him. "You featherbrain!" he yelled. "You crazy nitwit! What kind of a trick is that to pull on a fellow? You could have given me a heart attack!"

Now it was Jenny's turn to pull up short. "What are you talking about, Jerry? There were shark dorsal fins out there, three of them, coming straight for you!" Jenny was close to tears in her fright and frustration.

"Those weren't shark fins, you silly fool! They were dolphins, perfectly harmless dolphins!" Jerry's anger cooled and he began to relax. He was now feeling a bit guilty about shouting names at his sister. After all, they could have been sharks; there were plenty of them in these waters.

"But how did you know they were dolphins and not sharks?" quizzed Jenny, beginning to feel a bit sheepish. "After all, one big fish fin looks about the same as another out in the water like that."

"Dolphins aren't fish, Jenny, they're mammals. They have to come up to the surface and breathe air. That's how I knew they weren't sharks. I saw them leap into the air."

"Oh," said Jenny. She was beginning to feel a little stupid.

Suddenly Jerry pointed toward the beach and gave a yell. "Oh, no! Look where Becky and Dani are! They've gotten way ahead of us." The twins plunged toward the shore, grabbed up their sneakers and backpacks, yanked the kite spools from their positions in the seawall, and headed north up the beach at full gallop.

It took the kite racers the greatest portion of the morning to reach the beach house. Becky and Dani were still in the lead, but only by a few hundred feet. They probably would not have been able to maintain the lead if it weren't for the discomfort Jerry was experiencing from his gradually drying jeans. The sun and wind dried them into a salty stiffness that rubbed and chafed his legs. He knew he had to do something to remedy the situation or he would surely lose this race.

Jenny came up with the bright idea of calling their mom when they got to Becky's house. They would ask her to grab a change of clothing for Jerry and rush them down to him as fast as the car could get her there. Jerry would jump into the shower while they waited for her, and sometime within the break period he would grab a quick bite to eat.

The plan proved to be a good one and the twins were not far behind when the race resumed. This next lap would be easy. They were rested and refreshed, and the beach surface was clear and firm. It took them a little more than an hour to reach Pelican Pier on the northeastern tip of the island.

Now the entire nature of the race changed again. They had the tough terrain of the northern coastline to traverse. Becky and Dani noticed that the storm had laid down a thin strip of beachline at the base of the broken seawall. They decided to take this route rather than risk the briers and brambles that covered the land at the top of the seawall. The decision proved to be a major error.

Jerry and Jenny, still behind, decided to brave the prickly

area above the seawall. They both had blue jeans and heavy socks on, and felt that they could wade through the lower weeds and jump along the rocks to get around the higher brush.

Things went pretty well for both teams until they got around the curve and approached Sawgrass Bluff. Becky and Dani found that much of their narrow strip of sand was blocked by deadfalls. Old trees and broken limbs had been washed down the river by the storm and thrown up against the shore by the extremely strong currents and tidal waters that surged through the estuary. At first they tried climbing over them at first. But the further upstream they moved, the more numerous and tangled the roadblocks became. Then they tried climbing up the rocks of the old seawall to get around the bad spots. The rocks, however, were loose and slippery from clinging bits of seaweed and salt spray. Obviously they had to abandon the lower route and climb up to the top of the seawall.

They worked their way painfully up the sharp slippery rocks. It was not easy to control their kites, and they had to perform the whole maneuver in a series of relay movements. One girl would hold both kite spools while the other, grasping with both hands, climbed a few feet up the rocks. Then the spools would be handed up and the next girl clawed her way up the rocks. They were losing precious time!

By now the Red Bombers had made it to the bluff. There was a dense thicket of shrubs and underbrush growing up the steep north face of the bluff. They had to avoid that at all costs, for their kite strings would become hopelessly tangled. It was either edge their way along the rocks or climb the bluff. Jenny insisted on the latter and Jerry decided that she was probably right. They started up the hill.

It was then that they realized the difference in the air currents over this estuary mouth. Their kites jerked at the end of the flying lines. The upper air currents, like the water currents below, were much stronger and faster. It felt as though the kites would surely be torn right off the lines and swept across the estuary. Their arms ached with the tugging by the time they got to the top of the bluff.

Becky and Dani had been so preoccupied with their difficult climb up the face of the seawall that they were disoriented at first. They had been keeping their eyes on the twins' kites while they were walking along the north beach-line. Invariably the wind had pulled them to the west. Now they spotted the twins high up on the bluff, but where were their kites?

"Hey, Becky," shouted Dani. "The twins are way ahead of us, but I think they've lost their kites. This might be our race, after all!"

Becky tapped Dani on the shoulder and pointed to the north. There, like two colorful but distant birds, were the kites. "The air currents between these two islands must be something else again, Dani!" Becky started reeling in her kite as she spoke. "The twins are having a rough time controlling those kites and they may very well lose them. Let's reel our kites in as close to us as possible. Maybe we can keep them out of those strong air currents and increase our chances for recovering our losses."

The girls made quick time up the bluff, and they still had good control of their kites, though they were treacherously low to the ground. Jerry and Jenny were making their way across the little stream that emptied itself into the estuary. They had been slowed by the marshy area at the base of the bluff. Stands of razor-sharp sawgrass grew in this marshy area, and walking through it was far from comfortable; besides, it was slow. But the end of the race was in sight. There to the northwest was the bridge that connected Sanctuary Island to the next island north. Nothing short of a miracle would allow the girls to win the race now.

Dani voiced that thought as the girls headed down the west slope of the bluff. "Becky, do you think it would help to pray and ask God to help us win?"

Becky was silent for a moment. "Somehow, Dani, I don't think that's the right thing to pray for. It's sort of like asking

God to show favoritism. I mean, this isn't exactly a battle between good and evil. I think God just wants us to do the very best we can and be good sports, no matter who wins. Let's just keep going and try to finish the race. That alone will be a big accomplishment."

"Yeah," answered Dani, "when you look at it that way, I guess you're right. I sure did have my heart set on flying that big kite, though!"

The girls continued down the bluff and started through the sawgrass. They decided to move closer to the shoreline, where the sharp grass was not as thick. That brought them to the wide mouth of the little stream. They pulled off their sneakers and tied the laces together so they could hang the shoes around their neck. Because the streambed was quite deep and had a strong current here at the mouth, the girls knew they needed free hands and arms for better balance.

Dani was several paces behind Becky, watching her feel her way gingerly through the soft muck and weeds that clogged the bottom of the streambed and caused it to spread out like a miniature delta. She decided to follow Becky's footsteps as closely as possible; her greatest concern was the possible nibbles she might receive on her feet from crabs.

They were concentrating so hard on the task before them that Dani was momentarily stunned when Becky let out a piercing scream and suddenly seemed to disappear. It all happened in a split second. Dani heard a loud splash and realized that Becky had gone down, but not straight down. She was sliding along, trying to push herself back up and regain her balance, but it was impossible. She had stepped on a long sloping rock that was covered with a layer of mud and slippery weeds. It was like going down a steep poolslide that had water running down it.

Dani could only stand and watch, horror struck, as Becky was swept out of the streambed and into the swift currents of the estuary. Dani was totally helpless. She realized that, with one wrong step, she, too, could be carried out into the rushing deep waters.

Becky turned over in the water and started swimming for the shore as hard as she could. She was a strong swimmer. Having a pool in her backyard had given her plenty of practice. She was one of the few members of her Pathfinder Club who had earned the Advanced Swimmer's honor. She was also used to saltwater and ocean currents, for she had lived near the ocean all her life. But this was different. She could feel the tremendous power of the water, the estuary current sucking and pulling at her. Strength was not enough. Adrenalin surged through her body and she stroked and kicked with all her might, but it would not be enough. She knew it would not be enough! Still she pulled and kicked.

Dani had stepped backward onto firmer ground. She looked for something long enough to reach out toward Becky—a branch, a floating object, anything. But she could find nothing but the sharp edged sawgrass. She began to shout for help as loud as she could. The twins might hear her and come back. Perhaps together they could form a human chain. She prayed but she did not know what to ask for, other than that God would find a way to save her friend.

The twins, in the meantime, were approaching the bridge. They had only the last 200 or 300 feet of the seawall and the embankment at the end of the bridge to go. Jerry was elated. His eyes scanned the bridge for sight of his mother. He knew she would be waiting there, and he thought of how proud she would be. Then he saw her. She was running toward them, waving her arms and shouting. "Hey, Jenny," he called to his sister, "here come our cheering fans!"

But Jerry stopped when he made out the look on his mother's face. It was not happiness, or even excitement. It was sheer terror! What was wrong? What was she screaming?

Then, out of the corner of his eye, he saw a long, brightly colored object floating down to the water at the bottom of the seawall. It was Becky's kite. It gracefully sank downward and gently touched the surface of the water, the end of it's tail caught on a deadfall limb lying on the bank. For a moment he was at a loss as to what was happening. Something was terribly wrong, but what? Jenny's sudden shout, so close behind him, startled him. "Oh, no! Jerry—look, she's in the water! Becky has fallen into the water! She'll be swept right out with the current!"

The terrible reality of the situation suddenly seized him. What could they do? How could they get to her? They needed something long, like a rope. But he had no rope! There were only the kites and the thin kite lines. The flying lines were strong enough for lightweight kites, but not for a person caught in a strong current.

Suddenly the answer flashed to his mind. The kites! Becky's kite! He dropped the spool of his kite and jumped along the rocks of the seawall, going down fast and recklessly. In seconds he had reached the tail end of Becky's kite, untangled it, and drew it in. He grasped the bridle, tangled now in the flying line; he pulled the little jackknife from his pocket and cut the strings.

He could feel his heart racing and his breath coming in hard, sucking gasps as he ran down the beach toward the mouth of the little stream. His mind was racing with his body. How would he get the end of the tail out in the water to Becky? He needed something to tie onto it, something heavy enough to throw but light enough to float. The pieces of driftwood on the beach. That was it!

He never broke his stride but reached down as he ran and scooped up a chunk of driftwood, smoothed and softened by the water. He had reached the stream but Becky had been washed further down the estuary and he had to leap across, narrowly missing the slick submerged rock himself.

Dani was moving along the beach, shouting to Becky to keep swimming. Jerry reached her and showed her the long tail of Becky's kite. "Quick, Dani, hold this driftwood piece while I tie the kite tail around it." Then he positioned himself as closely in line with the struggling swimmer as possible.

"Jerry!" wailed Dani. "That kite tail is just heavy cellophane. Won't it tear when she pulls on it?"

Jerry glanced quickly at Dani's frightened face. "You're the one who knows how to pray. You better start praying that it doesn't tear."

His first throw fell short. He needed to move further down the bank. Wading into the water above his knees, he threw again. It was still a few feet short, but Becky understood. From somewhere within her exhausted muscles she gathered a new burst of energy. She put her face down into the water and stroked as hard as she could. Then her fingertips grasped at the soft driftwood and she curled her hand around it. Her burst of strength gave out. She could no longer pull; she could only hold on.

The exhausted relaxation of everything but her tightly gripped hand was the best thing that she could have done, though she didn't do it on purpose. Slowly and carefully Jerry and Dani drew in the kite's tail, trying not to jerk it or make any sudden moves. Becky was pulled closer and closer toward the shore. And then they had her! They grabbed her arm and pulled her onto the beach.

Mrs. Howard and Jenny, puffing and gasping for breath, came upon the three children sitting quietly on the beach. She heard Becky and Dani's prayer of thankfulness. Then she heard her son's "Thank you, Lord!" It was the first time that she had ever heard him pray.

* * * * *

Two sets of parents and an elderly woman sat on the Howards' back porch that evening and watched the stars glittering in a clear, blackened sky. The supper had been delicious. The four children sat on the wooden steps. Just above them, on the wide porch deck, lay a huge kite with a long rainbow tail curled around it. The dimmed house lights revealed a large, proud peacock strutting across the face of the kite, his brilliant tail spread to pick up the faintest rays of light. The children were talking quietly among themselves, and there seemed to be a difference of opinion.

"I think you two should get the kite," said the boy quietly. "After all, this whole kite race was your idea. You even came up with the idea for the prize."

"Yes," said his sister. "We want you to keep the kite. It will help to remind you of our lovely little sea island."

"No," answered Dani. "You would have won the race if you didn't have to drop your kite and turn back. We want you two to keep the kite."

Becky reached out and stroked the long ribbons of the folded tail. They felt silky and warm to her touch. It was such a beautiful kite! "It's yours, Jerry," she said with quiet firmness. "It's yours because now it's more than just a prize. It's also a reward."

Chapter 7

Sneaker Sucker Swamp

The little canoe carrying two young explorers through the deep woods and thickets that covered the western shore slipped through the quiet backwaters of Sanctuary Island. The girls had never seen this portion of the island, for there were no roads or trails here. If they had had some type of a motorized boat that could have taken them along the southern shore into Porpoise Fin Inlet, they might have approached the western side of the island, but even that would have been difficult.

The waterway between Sanctuary Island and the next little island to the west was, in reality, a large marsh. The marsh was covered with brackish water during high tide. When the tide was out, it was a land of sharply pointed spartina grass and thick mud. Not ordinary brown mud like you find after a hard rain or under melting snow, mind you. No, indeed; marsh mud is unique! First of all, it's very black and slimy. Secondly, it smells! If you disturb marsh mud by digging into it or squashing through it with your feet, you get the distinct odor of rotten eggs. This smell comes from decaying plant and animal matter that has been packed in sedimentary layers. When disturbed, it gives off a gas called hydrogen sulfide. Marsh mud is one of nature's most effective barriers against the casual tourist. Only the truly dedicated will venture through it!

The shoreline edges of the marsh, in turn, consisted of

another formidable barrier. A heavily vegetated swamp blends the marsh with the solid earth of the little island. The swamp is the home of many kinds of wildlife and is an important part of the ecology of both the island and the marsh. But both the swamp and the marsh are harsh environments and not easy places to travel through. It was this very environment that made the sea islands of the low country such wonderful hiding places for pirates and escaped slaves.

Becky and Dani thought of this as they paddled the little canoe along the creek. They had to keep pushing brush away from their watery path and, in some spots, hack through it with an old machete that they had found in a long-deserted boathouse. The machete and the canoe were proving to be the keys to unlock the mysteries of the western portion of the island.

The canoe was old and just big enough for the two of them, but it was sturdy and seaworthy. The Turtle Woman had loaned it to them for the summer. Neither of them were expert canoeists. Becky had spent some time learning the basics of canoeing during her first year as a Pathfinder. Dani had never been in a canoe before. But what the girls lacked in experience they made up for with determination and not a small amount of courage. They had spent several days of practice in the open portions of the creek that traversed the center of the island. Then they had gradually pushed westward. Going a little deeper into the thickets, they followed the creek as it meandered its way west.

Having to tunnel their way through the brush that choked the surface of the little waterway, after a week of slow progress they came to a fork in the creek. One branch headed directly south. The other branch went to the northwest. The northwestern branch was the widest and least clogged of the two, so the girls decided to try their chances in that direction first. They hadn't gone more than 100 feet or so when to their surprise the little creek made a sharp turn westward and opened out into a secluded lake. The waters of the lake were dark and quiet; a tiny island sat in its center. The island was just large enough to accommodate one huge old cypress tree. Its branches of feathery foliage spread down to a lush carpet of moss and ferns.

The girls were enchanted by this lovely spot. It was so quiet and peaceful, totally secluded even within the privacy of this small sea island. They knew immediately that this was to become their special little hideaway.

The lake was so small that its exploration took only some 10 or 15 minutes of paddling. But within that short time span they made two interesting discoveries. First, on the north shore they found the remains of an old boathouse, its sagging frame draped with vines and thick shrubs. They carefully maneuvered their small craft inside, where they found several old rusty tools hanging from the broken wall. A rusted machete was the only usable instrument, but it would take some time and elbow grease to clean, polish, and sharpen it.

The second discovery was more important, and they had almost overlooked it. They were slowly paddling along the western shoreline when they noticed a bubbling and rippling of the water in one spot under an especially thick cover of vegetation. They pulled and hacked away the thick vines and branches, thinking at first that they had found another creek emptying into the small lake. As they prodded their way through, they realized that the heavy shade was giving way to increasing rays of sunlight. Suddenly, like the parting of curtains, the brilliance of the blue summer sky was before them. And below it, rippling in waves like a windswept prairie, lay a beautiful expanse of salt water marsh. They had found it! They had found a way to the western shore of Sanctuary Island!

The girls sat in the canoe in stunned silence for some time. Their eyes had become so accustomed to the dark shade and thick shadows that the sudden burst of sunlight temporarily blinded them. As their eyes adjusted to the bright light, they saw beyond the expanse of marsh the outline of a small island to the west of Sanctuary Island. They had seen this little island on navigation maps of the area but couldn't recall if it even had a name. They did know, however, that it was only about one fourth the size of their island and was uninhabited.

Now there is something magnetic about an uninhabited island. Becky and Dani knew that they *had* to get there! They really weren't sure why. It's something like the reason for climbing a mountain. Ask a mountain climber why he wants to climb a mountain and he'll tell you, "Because it's there." The girls wanted to get to that island for the same reason, because it was there!

But finding an opening to the marsh that separated the two islands, and getting across it proved to be two very different things. The young explorers made many trips to the hidden lake, but they could find no way across the oozy mud and sharp spartina grass of the marsh. The exchange of waters between the lake and the marsh was like the action of a sponge. The pressure of the incoming tide did not provide enough water to cover the marsh. It only seemed to squeeze the brackish water into the little lake. Any water emptying itself from the lake at low tide was quickly absorbed by the marsh.

Finally the girls decided to give up their quest temporarily and just get to know their special hideaway. They tried coming at different times of the day and found it to be constantly changing. During the early morning hours, it was a place of riotous chirping and twittering. Birds in great number flocked to this area to greet the first rays of the sun. But it was the small herds of deer that the girls found most fascinating. If they entered the lake very quietly, moving into the wind, they would often see several graceful does with their young fawns following close behind on spindly legs. The deer came to the lake to drink and to feed on the lush green grasses that hung over the water's edge.

During the heat of the day, the lake and its shoreline would become quiet and appear to be almost deserted. Turtles and fish occasionally disturbed the water's surface, and on at least two visits the girls spotted alligators moving slowly along with only their snouts and eyes breaking the surface. But the two nature lovers knew that sleeping peacefully in and under the shadowy trees were many creatures of the nighttime hours. They longed to try coming here at night, or perhaps to camp overnight on the tiny islet in the center. But somehow, they never got up the courage. Their peaceful daytime hideaway would be far too frightening during the dark hours of the night!

But they did come in the early hours of the evening. It was then that they discovered the secret of the old cypress tree that stood on the tiny island. It was a warm summer evening when they made this latest discovery. They had let their canoe drift in toward the lake, trying to ignore the buzzing of mosquitoes and gnats. The last rays of the sun made a red glow through the trees along the western bank, and a slight breeze rustled through the encircling branches and vines. All was quiet and peaceful. The girls nestled down into the canoe and watched for the movements of the raccoon, deer, or other wildlife on the banks.

They were suddenly startled by a rushing sound in the sky. It seemed to be coming from the sunset itself. They heard the beating of many wings. The light in this secluded spot was growing very dim. It was an eerie sight that met their eyes when they looked upward. The nearly ghostlike forms of many large white birds came sailing in over the tree tops. With wings spread wide, they circled the old tree. One after another they glided to a roosting spot on the outspread branches. In a matter of minutes the entire tree was decorated with white feathery creatures. They looked like long blobs of snow that had been haphazardly dropped on the dark green branches. The girls were so awed by the sight that they simply sat and stared, reluctant to break the magic of moment.

Finally, Dani squeezed Becky's arm and asked in hushed tones, "What are they? I've never seen anything like that before. It's almost spooky!"

Becky shook her head in uncertainty. "I'm not sure, but I

think they're some kind of egret. I got a look at the heads of some of them. Their white plumage is something else!"

When they arrived back home, the girls got out their nature guides. Sure enough, Becky had been right. The birds were indeed egrets, not the great egret with long curving neck, but the snowy egret; their plumage was once highly prized and much sought after for women's bonnets. The girls discovered that these lovely birds had come close to extinction at the turn of the century, due to greedy plume-feather hunters. And so, Sanctuary Island was again living up to its name. Obviously it was a sanctuary for snowy egrets.

The naming of the lake and its little island was easy. The two young mapmakers added their latest discoveries to the map they had started at the time of the kite race. The name of Fawn Lake was now carefully drawn in. The little island probably had been created by silt and plant life catching around cypress knees over the years, gradually forming a piece of land known as a hammock. Thus the name Egret Hammock was an appropriate title.

There were still some blank spots on the map, however, and this bothered the girls. Where did the southern branch of the creek go? What was on the southwestern corner of Sanctuary Island? What was that uninhabited island to the west of Sanctuary Island like? There was only one way to find the answers to these questions. The young explorers would have to strike out in a new direction.

The girls awoke early one morning and packed their knapsacks. They put in a change of clothes, compass, map, plenty of extra pencils, a pair of binoculars, insect repellent, and a hearty lunch. They filled their canteens and wore their oldest sneakers and blue jeans. Exploratory research does not require high fashion. With their gear stowed in the bottom of the canoe, they set off. Today they would head down the southern fork of the creek.

They reached the branching of the creek just as the southern rays of a warm summer sun began to filter through the upper treetops. Dani was in the bow with the machete.

She really didn't need a paddle, as she would have no time to use it. Her job was to cut away the overhanging vines and branches and watch for submerged logs or rocks. Becky was in the stern, using J-strokes with her paddle so she could both steer a course and keep them moving forward. It was hard work for both of them and, after an hour of slow progress, they decided to rest a bit and then change places.

It was nearly one o'clock in the afternoon when they finally came into open water. They had been so involved in their efforts to clear a passage along the choked creek that they had totally forgotten about lunch. Now they were famished! They decided to search for a clear area of bank where they could get out and stretch their legs and eat their lunch in comfort.

They found an ideal spot when they came to a smaller creek entering from the west. It was so shallow that they had to move up it very slowly to avoid dragging the bottom of their canoe. But they were soon rewarded for their care and patience. Gradually the little brook widened and deepened and entered what could only be called a lagoon. It circled around several little marshy islands of tall grass. The banks were clear and covered with soft moss and low grasses. There was deep shade all around them; and the spot was cool, even though the August day was hot and humid.

The girls beached their canoe and stretched out on the cool grasses. What a lovely spot this was! They happily munched on their sandwiches and took long, refreshing sips of the fruit drinks they had in their thermoses. Then they lay back to relax. Both of them were asleep in minutes.

Becky awoke first. She rolled over, not remembering where she was at first. Her hand touched something long and furry. Involuntarily, she grasped it and then sat up with a jolt, "Yike! What is this?" she screamed.

Dani awoke with a start and stared at her friend. "What on earth are you screaming about? Are we under attack or something?" Her mouth fell open as she looked at the object in Becky's right hand. "Oh, dear, Becky, you've killed something!"

Becky dropped the furry object and jumped back. "Killed something! How could I have killed something when I was sound asleep? I just rolled over, and there it was. Hey, what is it, anyway?"

Dani picked up a branch and approached the long furry object. She prodded it several times and then lifted it with the branch. It was matted with mud and dried bits of grass and leaves and the girls could not identify it at first. Finally, Becky's curiosity got the best of her. She quickly grasped the object and dipped it in the lagoon several times.

What finally emerged was the tail of an adult raccoon. Obviously, it had been lying there for some time, for the amputated end was dried and shriveled. But the thick fur of the tail was in remarkably good condition, probably preserved by the heavy coating of swamp mud. "How on earth could a raccoon have lost his tail out here?" asked Becky. "Do you think trappers could have come into this area?"

Dani shook her head. "It's possible, I suppose, but they probably would have approached from the marsh. I don't think they would have risked coming across the bridge with the ranger's station so close by." Dani pondered the thought for a few seconds. "How would they come in through that marsh, though? The water level is so low and the mud is so thick, I don't think even airboats would work."

Becky looked doubtful. "Nope, I don't think it was trappers. That marsh is nothing but miles of sticky mud." She looked thoughtfully into the dark waters of the lagoon. "Hey, I bet I know what happened! An alligator bit it off, or maybe a snapping turtle."

A startled look came over Dani's face. Her eyes scanned the surface of the lagoon and she began backing away from the water's edge. "Hey, Becky, maybe this isn't such a great idea. I mean, there could be all kinds of gruesome creatures out here! Think of it. There are probably alligators watching us right now, and maybe water moccasins and rattlesnakes! I don't think I like this exploring business, after all." Dani was talking in a rapid, high-pitched voice by now, and she was close to panic.

"Calm down, Dani!" Becky had to shout to get Dani's attention. "You're making it much worse than it really is. Of course there are dangers out here. We just have to be very careful. No more going to sleep on the banks of a lagoon. We've got to stay alert. Come on, kiddo, don't chicken out on me now. We've come such a long way on our mapping of the island. This is really the last section that needs to be done. Please, Dani; maybe we can finish it off this afternoon. There are still a few hours of sunlight left. Why, I bet we're nearly to the southwest corner now. Let's just continue on down the creek a little way and see."

Dani was regaining her composure and her adventuresome spirit was returning. A slow smile spread across her face as she looked at the raccoon tail that Becky still held. It would make a lovely trophy! "Get out the map, Becky. I've just thought of a great name for this lagoon." Dani carefully penciled in the name, Coon Tail Lagoon.

They climbed back into the canoe and paddled southward down the creek. The going became much easier as the tangle of overhanging brush and deep woods gave way to a swampy area. Stately cypress trees covered with waving beards of Spanish moss dominated the swamp. The girls had to be careful of the rounded projections of cypress knees, which could tip over their canoe if hit just right.

They could still see the deep channel of the creek as it cut through the swamp, and they tried to stay within it. The water level in the main body of the swamp was quite low, probably too low for their canoe. To the east of the creek was a low ridge of dry land that widened and supported thicker vegetation.

They hadn't gone far when they noticed another small branch of water emptying into the creek in a southwesterly direction. Sizing up the depth of the water, they decided to risk their canoe in this narrow branch. To their delight, it too

opened up into another lovely little pond with slick mud banks.

There was a loud splash from the far bank as the canoe nosed its way into the pond. The girls saw gradually widening ripples of water moving outward from the bank. Something had obviously just made a quick dive. Suddenly, a sleek brown object slid down the muddy bank of the opposite shore and slipped, with barely a splash, into the dark waters.

Otters! The girls had discovered an otter slide! They gently pushed their canoe back into the covering brush of the small creek and sank down quietly to watch the show. They had all they could do to keep themselves from laughing out loud, for they suddenly found that they were spectators at a circus. Possibly no other creature in nature enjoys play quite as much as the otter. An entire troop of little otter clowns began cavorting before the twinkling eyes of the concealed audience of two. The girls spent more than half an hour watching the show. They would have stayed longer but they were both getting stomachaches from holding their giggles, and cramped muscles from trying to stay hidden in the bottom of their little canoe.

Reluctantly they pushed the canoe backward until they were once again in the main creek. Becky turned around and looked into Dani's face. Then, like the sudden bursting of a flood-swamped dike, peals of laughter shattered the encircling silence. The girls laughed until tears streamed from their eyes and they were gasping for breath.

"Whew!" gasped Becky when she finally gained some measure of control. "I sure needed that laugh. What a relief to get it out!"

Dani was too exhausted even to answer. She lay her paddle down and slumped back into the canoe till only her arms and legs were hanging over the sides in total relaxation. Becky slumped down beside her for she, too, felt very tired. Everything became quiet again, except for an occasional little unwinding sort of giggle. The girls felt intoxicated by the pleasure of the otter circus and the warm southern sun that filtered through the treetops.

The gentle breeze rocked the little canoe as it floated free. The buzzing of insects and the twittering of birds lent a feeling of complete peace. What a lovely way to spend a warm summer afternoon! The girls' previous caution was lulled to sleep with them. They didn't feel the little jolts as their craft floated its way into the swamp, gently bumping from one tree to another. Besides, the tide was going out and the swamp was gradually being drained. Soon the canoe was nicely snuggled into a blanket of soft, warm mud. Perfect peace reigned—until a cloud of mosquitoes discovered the meal awaiting them in the canoe!

Dani awoke with a painful start. She looked with amazement at the red welts that already covered the exposed soft skin of her forearm. "Yikes!" she screamed with genuine fear. "I'm being eaten alive! I'm being carried away by a cloud of mosquitoes! Becky, do something."

But Becky had her hands full trying to fend off the stinging attackers herself. "There's an army of them, Dani! Look out, I'm going to use the bug spray." She stood up in the well-anchored canoe and began spraying frantically in all directions. A suffocating cloud of repellent replaced the cloud of mosquitoes.

Coughing and gasping for air, Dani reached through the haze of spray and grabbed Becky's arm. "Stop, Becky, stop! You'll kill us along with the mosquitoes!" The two girls collapsed into the canoe, sneezing and rubbing their smarting eyes.

"Wow, Becky! You had me scared for a minute there. I thought that horde of mosquitoes was using chemical warfare."

"Well, I did warn you," answered Becky. "Look at you. You look like one big red welt. I think we'd better get out of here before they send out their reserve troops." She stuck her hand over the side of the canoe to wash off the repellent. A startled expression came over her face and she slowly lifted her hand up. She examined it as though it were a strange object and not one of her own appendages.

Dani glanced over and her mouth dropped open. "What's that slimy black stuff all over your hands?" she asked.

"I don't know," answered Becky. "It looks like mud. It came from down there." She pointed with a muddy forefinger over the side of the canoe.

Dani pulled herself upright and looked over the side of the canoe. She let out a startled gasp. "What happened to the water? Where's the creek?" Then, realization of their predicament struck her with such a force that she could barely speak. All attempts at humor were gone. They were in deep trouble. Not only was the canoe hopelessly mired in thick mud, the sun was getting low and long shadows were turning the swamp into a place of eerie half-light. The waving gray moss now clung like threatening webs, grasping towards the canoe, trying to hold it fast from above just as the mud was doing from below. The sound of large wings could be heard in the tops of the cypress trees. The daytime silence of the swamp was fading with the approach of evening. The air began to move and cool with a freshening breeze, and the swamp seemed to be coming to life. Night, in the swamp, is the time of the hunters.

"Uh-oh," whispered Dani. "Maybe we're going to camp out overnight after all."

"Maybe you are," answered Becky, trying to keep the sound of panic out of her voice, "but I'm not! I'm getting out of here if I have to wade through mud up to my arm pits!"

"Are you kidding!" exclaimed Dani. "You would actually consider stepping out of this canoe and walking through that slimy muck in the dark? You must be out of your mind!"

"Well," retorted Becky, "it's either wade through mud or swing through the trees. Besides, it's not quite dark yet. Maybe we can find the creek bed while there's still a little light left. "We'll pull the canoe with us."

Dani knew that Becky was right. It was the only solution and they didn't have time for argument. The light was fading fast. The two girls took the time for a quick prayer for deliverance and gingerly climbed over the sides of the canoe. They sank into oozy mud up to their knees. They tried lifting their feet to walk but it was impossible. The movement of their feet caused a sickening sort of sucking noise. The only way to make progress was to push their feet forward and attempt to slide their legs through the muck. Forward progress could be measured only in inches.

A thick fog began to creep through the encircling trees, and the sulfurous rotten-egg smell of the disturbed mud was almost nauseating. The girls could see a raised ridge of what appeared to be solid ground ahead, but the thickening fog made it difficult to judge its distance.

Suddenly Dani let out an ear-piercing scream. "My sneakers! Something pulled my sneakers off!"

"It's the mud," gasped Becky. "I can feel it sucking at mine too. We'll be lucky if we lose just our sneakers. If we don't find that creek bed soon I'm going to lose my sanity!"

"But what if I step on su-su-something gruesome?" stuttered Dani.

"If it's alive, ask it where the creek is!" Becky didn't mean to be crude. She was trying her best to keep some humor in the situation. It seemed to be the only way to avoid complete panic.

They continued inching their way toward the ridge of land until they began to realize that they weren't sinking in as deeply and there was a solid sort of feeling under their feet. With a last desperate effort they lurched forward and pulled themselves up onto solid ground. Terra firma! Their bodies were covered with mud but it didn't matter. They looked down at their feet. Sure enough—no sneakers. The swamp had eaten them! But not even that mattered. They didn't need sneakers now. There, on the other side of the ridge of land, lay the dark waters of the creek.

It took only seconds to pull the canoe over the bank and slide it down into the welcoming water. They slipped into its recesses and felt the reassuring rocking movement under them.

They were enveloped in mist and gathering darkness as they paddled against the familiar current. But the darkness no longer frightened them. It was a part of this sea island world of salt marshes and swamps. They had conquered their fear and learned something important about themselves. They had learned of an inner strength, a God-given power that could sustain them even in the times of deep peril.

Dani began to recite a passage that had come to mind. It was a quote from the Ninety-first Psalm: "He who dwelleth in the secret place of the Most High shall abide under the shadow of the Almighty . . . Thou shalt not be afraid for the terror by night . . ."

Becky finished it: "He shall call upon me, and I will answer him. I will be with him in trouble; I will deliver him."

Chapter 8

A Sanctuary of Worship

The isolation of the little sea island, bravely facing the vast Atlantic Ocean and with miles of salt marsh at its back, was a very real attraction to Becky's family. Even their trips in early March, when the remnants of winter still held the land and sea in its grip, held special joy and fascination for them. The island looked so lonely and lost amidst the brown and gray shades of land and water. But the loneliness was a welcome contrast to the rush and bustle that they lived in the rest of the year, and even the somber colors were somehow relaxing after the constant tropical lushness of southern Florida.

Sabbath was a special time of peace and contentment. With the beauty of creation all around them it was easy to feel awe and reverence for the Creator. They enjoyed devising their own Sabbath school and worship services. There was no real formality to it. Formality was not necessary.

A favorite spot for meditation and worship was the elevated deck that looked out over the beach and the ocean to the east. The view from the deck was always lovely. But during the early morning hours of the Sabbath it somehow held a special attraction. The first rays of the sun spread a glowing light in the eastern sky and then turned the waters of the ocean into molten gold. Like the colors of the rainbow, the dawning of a new Sabbath day always held a special promise for those who had learned the beauty of its meaning.

During their first few weeks on the island, the family was content with this Sabbath isolation. But gradually the desire grew for fellowship with other Sabbathkeepers. Becky's mom often talked about Mrs. White's vision of looking over the earth and seeing glowing lights where companies of believers were located. Were there any glowing lights here along this rural coastline, they wondered?

They spent several weeks trying to find out. First, they checked the local phone books for Seventh-day Adventist churches, but found none listed. They traveled 30 miles to the nearest sizable town and began asking around. No luck! Then they checked the phone books of towns to the west. Still nothing. After several side trips and long-distance phone calls they found a large Seventh-day Adventist church in a city to the north. There was only one problem. It was 80 miles from the island's nearest town and more than 100 miles from Sanctuary Island. It would mean a round trip of 200 miles to attend church! They decided to continue having their own services.

But that didn't mean that they couldn't make an effort to spread the light in their own area. After all, their tiny group was, in effect, one of those little glowing lights, even though it might be no bigger than a spark. Sparks can turn into bonfires, given the right conditions.

They began to carry a supply of pamphlets and small booklets around with them in their travels. Pamphlets with offers for free Bible correspondence courses were left in phone booths; on newspaper and magazine stands in laundromats, beauty parlors, barber shops, and bus stations; and on park benches. They were seeds planted in new soil, and the Lord would nurture them in His own special way.

What the family did not know was that they were not alone in the planting of spiritual seed in this rich coastal land. They did not know that there were already two groups of Sabbathkeepers in that area, separated only by a river.

As a matter of fact, there was a period of time when the two little groups had not even known about each other.

There was a perfectly good bridge that crossed the river that separated them. But the Lord had waited for a spiritual bridge to be built before He could bring them together. Physical bridges made of steel and concrete work quite well for cars and trucks. But the hearts and minds of people that have been separated by social class, racial differences, and a lack of understanding for the needs of others require a much different sort of a bridge. Only Christ can provide the connecting link of deep love for one's fellowman.

One of the two little groups was made up predominantly of White folk that lived in the town and its suburbs. They met in the back of a bank on the west side of the bridge. The other little group was made up mostly of Black folk. They were hardworking farmers and laborers, with a scattering of college-trained professionals. They met in a home on the east side of the bridge.

Each group hoped to have its own church building some-day. But their numbers were small and there were no large amounts of money available, either. Buying a piece of property would be very expensive, let alone putting up even a small sanctuary. Neither group could see their way clear for such a project.

But the Lord was with each of these little groups of Sabbathkeepers, and He was working things out in His own time and in His own way. He knew that they had to recognize their dependency on Him. More than that, they had to recognize their need for each other and be willing to accept each other as brothers and sisters in Christ. There could be no social or racial prejudices. God wanted them to be one unit, working together for His glory. Then the seed could grow in fertile ground. Then the church could grow and take in new members, for its congregation would be ready to nurture them.

And when the time was right, they met. The group meeting on the island to the east of the bridge heard of the group meeting in the bank. They began to meet together and they accepted each other with joy. With their new unity they found strength, and a stronger desire to have their own sanctuary for worship.

Now the Lord was ready to show the power of His love in a very special way. The small congregation thought that it would be several years before they could save enough money to build their church. But God has all kinds of answers to our problems, even though we may think that there is only one solution.

The answer came in human form. A building contractor and his family were traveling through the South on their vacation. When they came through the coastal area of South Carolina they decided to find a church to worship in on Sabbath morning. They heard of the group meeting in the bank building and decided to join them.

The prayers that Sabbath morning were the same as the prayers of previous Sabbaths. The elder asked the Lord to bless them and to help them collect the funds they would need to build their sanctuary. The building contractor listened with interest. Here was a real opportunity for true missionary work! He thought of this large rural area that so much needed the message of God's remnant church. The Lord was speaking to his heart, and he was listening.

Now this man was no ordinary building contractor. He specialized in prefabricated buildings. He had the manpower, the finances, and the equipment readily available in the northern state where he lived. God, as usual, had the perfect man who was needed for the job.

What joy there was in the basement of that bank building as the contractor revealed his plans for this special little group of God's children! They were to pool their resources and find a plot of land for their new church. Then they would work together to clear the land and prepare the cement-slab floor and foundation. The prefabricated sanctuary would be brought down from the north on large flatbed trucks and assembled on the foundation. It was hard to imagine that they would really have their own church, not in a matter of years but in only a few months!

Becky's dad was the first of his family to discover the new church. This was their fourth spring vacation on the island, and by this time they were seriously looking around at real estate. They were not in a position to do any moving yet. Both of Becky's parents were self-employed and had worked too hard to establish their business in Florida to simply walk away from it now. But they were thinking of buying some land in the hope of a more rural home for the future.

Dad had been making side trips on his own, looking at available properties on other islands along the coastal area. He had worked his way closer to the main town and was now heading down a little side road that he had traveled last year. The real estate agent had told him of some wooded lots that had just become available, some five miles down this road. There was a sharp turn in the road and then a stretch of woods. Dad remembered that there were a few lovely brick homes set back under the trees along this stretch, so he drove slowly, on the look out for "For Sale" signs. He wasn't really in a position to buy a house, but it wouldn't hurt to look.

Suddenly he spotted a very familiar-looking sign. It had a globe of the world on one end and the words "Seventh-day Adventist Church" plainly marked in the middle. Sure enough, there under the old live oaks stood a lovely little sanctuary building. It looked fresh and new, but the dirt driveway and parking lot gave ample evidence that it was well used. He was positive that it hadn't been there last summer!

When the family heard the news of his discovery they could hardly wait to see for themselves. Mom decided that she did need to do some shopping in town after all, even though Dad had been very careful to get everything on the shopping list she had given him the day before. Becky and Dani decided that they really should come along to provide moral support. Besides, they might have the chance to visit their favorite toy store again.

By three o'clock that afternoon they were heading down

the little country road, scanning the sides for the familiar sign. Dad had said that they would make a sharp turn to the left and go along a wooded stretch.

"There it is!" shouted Becky suddenly. "It's over there on the right."

They started to pull into the dirt driveway when they saw a station wagon just backing out from beside the church. A young Black woman was driving, and there were four children in the car with her. She pulled to a stop when she noticed the van entering the drive, and a broad smile crept across her face. Neither group knew each other; they had never met before. But there was an immediate recognition. Each group knew that the others were brothers and sisters in Christ.

"Hi, there!" said the Black woman with a friendly wave of her hand. "I'm the church school teacher. You just caught us on our way home."

"My!" exclaimed Becky's mom. "Do you mean to tell me that you already have a church school going here? We just discovered this lovely little church. It surely hasn't been here very long, has it?"

"Just a few months," laughed the teacher. "And what you see in this car is the entire student body and teaching staff of our school. Two of the children are mine."

By this time everyone was out of the cars and greeting each other like old friends. Becky's mom told the teacher of their search for a church in the area and of how they had all but given up when they had accidently stumbled right onto it. She noticed the gleam in the teacher's eye as she looked at Becky and Dani. She was obviously ready to start looking for two more desks.

Becky's mom chuckled and told her that they would definitely be here for next Sabbath's services, but that they were visiting from Florida. They had only one week left of their vacation. How they would love to stretch that week to include a few more Sabbaths! Somehow, they could feel the warm friendliness of this little church even before meeting the rest of the congregation.

And so, on the last Sabbath of that vacation, a happy family climbed into their van and headed for a real church service in a real sanctuary. The inside of the little church looked almost miniature when they entered it. They were used to a large, high-ceiling church with well-spaced pews, a wide rostrum flanked by a piano and organ, and separate areas for Sabbath school classes and fellowship activities.

Here the pews were snuggled closely together and the ceiling was low. There was no organ, but there was a piano. A young Black man sat at that piano, playing with all his heart and soul. Even the very walls seemed to ring with the resounding joy of the instrument. Segregation did not exist in this church; it was utterly impossible for it to exist. Every pew was packed tightly. The congregation somehow managed to make room for a few more, though. They just put their arms around their neighbors' shoulders, and sure enough, one or two more people could be squeezed into the pew. This was definitely a church of togetherness!

One of the laymen of the church was the speaker for that day. They didn't have their own pastor, as yet. But every other week a pastor drove the long distance from his other church to present the sermon here. He must have used a lot of gas in the course of one month!

The sermon that day was beautiful in its simplicity and sincerity. The subject was love—God's love for His people, and His desire that His people learn to love one another in the same way. It was obviously straight from the heart and couldn't have been presented better by a practiced evangelist. The little family from Florida listened in awe. They had found a home away from home, a true sanctuary filled with the presence of God. They knew that this church would grow.

Sure enough, on their next trip back to Sanctuary Island they found another building going up behind the sanctuary. It was not a hall for the entertainment and social activities of the church. Obviously, this congregation had a distinctive set of priorities. The new building was to be a center where the church family could share their love with the surrounding community. It was appropriately called an "I Care Center" and would house the community service work, health education classes, and other community outreach programs.

The seeds had fallen on fertile ground, and they were growing. There were still problems to be solved. The congregation was not wealthy, and employment was scarce in the area. The members worried about this, for they were constantly losing new members or young people who had to move elsewhere to find work. But perhaps that too was part of the Lord's plan for this church family. Wherever these converts and young people traveled, they would carry the seed. The little flame was spreading.

The family talked of this on their way home to Florida. They saw in their minds' eye a long stretch of tidal coastline and beautiful sea islands in the darkness of night. Then a spark or two began to gleam through the darkness. The sparks grew brighter and began to merge, sending a warm glow of light that spread like the rays of morning sunshine, turning the ocean waves to gold. A new sanctuary had arrived—a sanctuary of worship to the Creator of all this beauty!

Chapter 9

Raccoon Rampage

No one could live on Sanctuary Island for very long without discovering which portion of the population really owned the island. It was definitely the raccoon clan! Their numbers were staggering to the imagination and, due to the vast food supply, their average adult size was prodigious. New human residents to the island soon learned that the words "raccoon" and "respect" were just about synonymous. If you had a raccoon in residence on your property, *he* was definitely the boss!

This especially held true for any garbage cans that might be placed on your lot. They were, in fact, food receptacles for raccoons. You could place spring locks on the lids, surround them with fences, bury them in ground containers—none of this fazed the raccoon in the least. Invariably the cans' contents would be strewn everywhere by morning. If raccoons have any inalienable rights, the freedom to all garbage cans is definitely one of them!

Becky's mom discovered this in no uncertain terms on her family's very first night on the island. She also learned an unforgettable lesson on when, and when not, to take out the garbage. The whole incident started quite innocently with a bit of house cleaning.

The family had just arrived and found that the previous renters had left quite a number of food items in the kitchen cabinets. Some of them, such as a can of evaporated milk and a small container of salt, were still usable. Others, such as a partially used bag of sugar, complete with resident ants, and a box of stale crackers, were definitely on the list of "things to be thrown out."

It was almost dark when the family arrived, and they all set to work at their assigned tasks so that they could relax for the evening. They had just made a 12-hour drive to reach the island. Becky was unpacking her suitcase and a large box of games, books, and other necessary items and was stowing things away in the front bedroom, which she was to occupy. Dad was unloading suitcases, boxes, bicycles, and the like from the car. Mom was cleaning out cabinets and storage places to make room for the things that were being moved in.

By nine p.m. the large plastic garbage bag of "things to be thrown out" was full to overflowing, but everyone was too hot, tired, and hungry to do the job. They decided to relax and have a bite to eat. The family sat around the kitchen table, eating sandwiches and talking about the things they wanted to see and do while they were on the island.

Becky could hardly wait to start looking for animals. She especially wanted to see raccoons. Ever since Dad was Becky's age he had had an unaccountable desire to have a pet raccoon, and he was encouraging her all the way. He had some vague memory of seeing a boy walk down his street with a friendly little raccoon on a leash, riding on his shoulder. He was sure that the sweet and cuddly little things would make wonderful pets.

Mom, on the other hand, tried to point out the facts as she had heard them. She also had some vague childhood memories of a neighbor with a pet raccoon, but her memories did not include the adjectives "sweet" or "cuddly"—they were more like "huge" and "vicious." She seemed to remember that this same neighbor had the tips of two of his fingers missing and the pet raccoon had had something to do with their loss. She also reminded her family that some raccoons carried rabies and there was an epidemic of that very disease in several neighboring states.

Nevertheless, everyone agreed that raccoons were certainly fascinating creatures and would be fun to watch. Becky hoped that they might have a few in the woods around the house and decided that she would try to find some tracks the very next morning. With that thought in mind, she headed into her bedroom to make sure that she hadn't forgotten the plaster of paris she would need to make casts of the tracks.

Dad was too tired to do any more unloading of the car and went to take a long, refreshing shower. That left Mom to take out the garbage. She didn't want to leave that bag of sugar, with its colony of ants, in the kitchen all night. She pulled on a bathrobe and slippers, grabbed the garbage bag and a large flashlight, and headed out the door. There was only one small problem—where were the garbage cans? Surely with a little searching she could find them.

The beam of the flashlight moved along the walls of the house. No garbage cans were visible. Then Mom searched the carport area under the house. She found a rusty shower and stumbled over some lawn chairs, but still no garbage cans. Well, there obviously had to be garbage cans somewhere. She certainly didn't want to leave this bag right out in the open where animals could scatter its contents everywhere. (At this stage of the game she was still very ignorant about raccoons and garbage cans!)

Finally the beam of her light landed on a wooden fenced-in area some 30 feet from the house. Maybe that was it. Still clutching the bag of garbage, she pushed through the bushes till she found a high wooden gate with a most efficient-looking latch. She pushed down on the latch and aimed her light tentatively into the small cubicle. Eureka! There sat three shiny metal garbage cans, their lids tightly in place.

Now, Becky's mom had long since overcome her childhood fear of the dark. After all, she was a grown woman! But a little twinge of something akin to fear began to creep down her spine. She hesitated in the gateway and directed the flashlight all along the inner walls of the fence. It was a high fence, probably about five and a half to six feet—definitely taller than she was. The lower limbs of a pine tree blocked out any view of the sky. A thick carpet of pine needles covered the ground in and around the fenced cubical, cushioning the sound of her steps.

Oh, well, she might as well get this job done and get back inside the cozy and well-lit house. She could hear the water running in the shower and her husband whistling a happy little tune. This creepy feeling that something was watching her was just plain silly!

She stepped into the cubicle and tried to lift the lid off the nearest garbage can. It seemed to be stuck tight! Well, she'd have to set down the flashlight and pull with both hands. She placed the light on the top of the next garbage can cover, braced her knees around the can she was trying to open, and gave a mighty pull on the lid. The lid flew off with such force that the two other garbage cans fell over and the flashlight fell to the ground. It rolled through the narrow space under the fence, but its beam was still shining into the cubicle. As a matter of fact, the light was shining directly toward the half-open gate.

A slight creaking sound from the gate made Mom turn around and look in that direction. Suddenly, the cold twinge of fear turned to outright terror! There, reflected in the weak beam of the light, were four pairs of slanting green eyes. There was dead silence and not even a blink from those eyes for several seconds. Then a low, heart-stopping growl came from the direction of the eyes.

Trapped! She was trapped in a little cubicle made of six-foot-high fencing, with four wild beasts at the gate and her flashlight out of reach! She could scream, but by this time her husband was singing lustily and would probably never hear her. Her 9-year-old daughter was in the house, but the mother instinct of not wanting her child attacked by wild creatures was too strong. Her mind raced through every possible escape route. Maybe she could jump the fence. Nope, not even adrenalin would get her over that fence before her attackers could reach her!

Then she remembered the bag of garbage. Maybe she could try diversionary tactics! Slowly she reached down into the bag, keeping her eyes riveted on the green slanting eyes gleaming evilly at her from the gate. Digging deep into the bag, she finally felt the box of stale crackers. She drew it out slowly and grabbed a handful. They felt rather soggy, but what do wild animals know about crackers? She cautiously threw the crackers towards the gate.

Four pairs of green shining eyes flashed downward and a wild chorus of grunting, snarling, and growling began. That was it! She could take no more! A shrill scream split the air.

Becky came flying around the side of the house with a large flashlight and a broom. Dad was just a few feet behind, wrapped in a large towel and brandishing a golf club. They raced in the direction of the scream, braced for mortal combat.

But they stopped short when they reached the gate of the garbage area. There, huddled under the gate, were four pathetically frightened little raccoons, with the remains of soggy and crumbled crackers scattered around them. They were literally frozen with fright! Becky cautiously peered into the fenced-in area. There sat her mother on one of the garbage cans, a look of abject terror on her face!

It was weeks before Becky let Mom live that one down. "Just imagine, Mom," she laughed. "You'll be able to tell everyone that you saved yourself from a wild pack of vicious rabid raccoons with a bag of garbage! I love it!"

"Very funny!" fumed Mom. "It was a pack and they could have been rabid, you know!"

That was the beginning of their adventures with raccoons. Soon they would grow to know and love them in a very special way. But, they would always respect them for the wild creatures that they were. There were some, however, that they came to know better than others, for their personalities were so distinctive.

The family's favorite raccoon was a large and feisty female named Cooky. They christened her with that name when they discovered that she was hooked on cookies. Her favorite were the sandwich kind, with cream filling. She would grasp them in her hand-like forepaws, sit back on her haunches with her tail protruding forward of her fat tummy, and carefully work the two outer cookies apart. Then, just like the average child, she would lick off all the filling. Finally she devoured the cookie sections themselves. She was so possessive of these special delicacies that she would fight off her own children to avoid having to share a single morsel.

Now at this point, a word must be said about the feeding of raccoons. The "experts" do not recommend it. Feeding raccoons, or any wild animal, by hand is definitely out. It is said that raccoons should not become used to human food handouts because their natural diet is far better for them. This premise can hardly be disputed. Becky's family tried to adhere to this rule—at first.

But where raccoons and humans share the same few miles of earth, the rule becomes pointless. Human food almost invariably becomes a part of the animals' diet. It's simply a matter of availability! If food does not come in the form of a freshly prepared meal, it will come in its partially decayed form as found in garbage cans. Becky's family found this out very quickly after spending a few mornings picking up the remnants of strewn garbage. They decided that freshly prepared food, conveniently placed in an area that was easily hosed down in the morning, would be a much preferable alternative.

They began cooking an extra pot of rice, buying whole watermelons, and keeping table scraps fresh until the raccoons' sunset dinner hour. The feast was placed on the back porch steps, along with a large bowl of water to accommodate the raccoon's peculiar food-washing (actually "food-feeling") habit. There were two large panes of glass on either side of the well-lighted porch door. The family could then station themselves behind these windows and watch the ensuing feeding frenzy in ease and safety.

Cooky began bringing her family of four pudgy babies to this feeding station during that first vacation. As a matter of fact, it was probably her babies who were involved in the great garbage can caper that first evening. But Becky's mom soon forgave them for that little indiscretion, for they became such adorable pests.

The peak of the house roof was split by high, narrow windows that provided extra sunlight in the high-ceilinged living room. These windows were a favorite late night spot for the Cooky family. If lights were on in the living room, moths and cicadas would be attracted to the outside of these windows. The little raccoons delighted in trying to catch them, as this, in fact, was really a part of their natural diet. Their little paws could be both seen and heard as they smeared bugs all over the glass. Any unsuspecting soul who sat alone in the living room late at night could receive quite a start when the scratching noise and the apparition of masked faces suddenly appeared in the high windows.

Mama raccoon took to sleeping on the peak of the house during the day. She would straddle the ridge with her fat body and watch Becky's family in their comings and goings. She became quite possessive of them (or perhaps it was of their food supply!). If the mood struck her she would waddle down the roof to the tall pine tree that touched the edge of the roof near the back door. Then she would peak at Becky and give her most provocative "Is-it-time-to-eat-yet?" look. During one of her descensions Becky managed to snap a picture of her. Mom had it enlarged so Becky could hang it on her bedroom wall.

Another raccoon with real personality was Tubblet. Tubblet had more fat on one body than two ordinary raccoons put together. From behind he looked like a brown blimp with a tail. His territory and feeding grounds included the front porch and he defended it like a wild boar! His meal always had to be prepared first. It consisted of a large roasting pan filled with rice, cheese, bread, table scraps, and anything that could be borrowed or begged from the neighbors.

This overweight ball of fur and fat had a special technique for guarding his food until he had eaten his fill. He would waddle up to the roasting pan, circle it once or twice like a bomber coming in for a landing, and then lie down full length in the pan so that his prodigious body covered the food. Then he would start eating his way backward, gradually moving his body back and over the end of the pan. It was a very efficient system, and there was usually nothing but crumbs left at the end of his meal.

During his entire feeding process, Tubblet kept one eye on the porch steps. If so much as one little black nose poked itself over the top step, Tubblet would growl, grunt, and hiss so loudly and ferociously that the intruder quickly backed off.

The best part of observing Tubblet at meal time was watching him try to get back down the steps. Actually, one could feel him go down the steps. The whole porch vibrated! He would take one step at a time, his legs flailing outward to accommodate his stomach, which bounced from one step to the next. The sound went something like this—"clomp, clomp, *thud.*" The clomps were the noise of his paws and the thud was his stomach landing on the next step.

Raccoons are territorial and have a well-established pecking order. The animals at the bottom of that order are usually the last ones to eat unless they are quick enough with the "hit and run" technique. This requires a great deal of bravery and often the risk of severe injury. Becky's family was often awakened by the sound of battle on the front or back steps at night. It was not uncommon to find bloody paw prints the next morning.

But these delightful masked bandits of the animal kingdom are also very sociable and family oriented. They take good care of their young, and father raccoon often takes his role of parenting very seriously. He is guardian and protector of his brood.

Becky and Dani discovered one such close knit family on a warm summer evening as they were hiking through the high-ground wooded area in the northwest section of the island. They were climbing a steep rise when they heard a high-pitched chirring sound. Obviously it was a warning signal. When they reached the top of the rise they could look down into a lovely little wooded dell. It was a well-protected spot and offered lots of cover for any wildlife that might choose that area for a home.

The girls would have missed the raccoon family entirely if one of the little ones had not chosen that moment to let out a plaintive little call of fright. A tall, graceful tree stood in the center of the dell, its upper branches almost at the same level as the top of the steep hill that Becky and Dani were standing on. In the fading evening light the girls saw three little forms hanging onto the ends of the thin upper branches of one side of the tree. On the other side of the tree sat the large forms of Mama and Papa Raccoon.

The little one that had been calling for help had gotten too far out onto the end of a thin branch. The branch was swaying up and down precariously, and baby raccoon seemed in eminent danger of losing his hold. This set the other two babies to wailing. Mama and Papa, putting aside their fear of the approaching humans, began working their way toward their bawling brood, clucking gentle sounds of encouragement as they drew closer. The babies were obviously heartened by the closeness of their parent. They stopped their crying and began to pull themselves upward on the branches, inching closer to Mama and Papa.

Within a few minutes the little family had worked itself together onto the firm central branches of the tree. Then, with great dignity and a haughty disregard for the intruding humans, they climbed down the tree in an orderly line until the whole family had reached the ground. Without even turning back once to look over their shoulders, Papa, Mama and three baby raccoons walked slowly off into the underbrush and disappeared.

Chapter 10

Heat Wave!

The girls sprawled themselves on the top step of the long flight of wooden stairs that led to the beach. The tide was coming in and gentle waves were already lapping at the bottom step. There were no white-crested breakers today. Even the ocean had been subdued by the oppressive heat that covered the southeastern states like a giant electric blanket. The state of South Carolina seemed to be the bull's eye of this heat wave. It was being called the worst heat wave and drought in the history of the state.

No appreciable rain had fallen in more than a month, and meteorologists said that they saw no signs of rain for the immediate future. Lakes, ponds, and streams were drying out, and even the underground water levels were at a dangerous low. Water restrictions had been put into force in many counties, and there was talk of mandatory statewide water restrictions.

To make matters worse, the temperatures had been above 100 degrees every day for more than two weeks; and the humidity was more than 90 percent. The news seemed to get worse every day; more and more deaths were reported due to the stifling heat. As usual, the toll was worst among the old and poor. Many of these folks depended upon their little garden plots for food. But even the weeds were dying!

The devastating extent of the heat and drought could most easily be seen in the state's farmlands. The corn crop was drying up without even producing mature ears. Hay for the cattle was virtually nonexistent. The pitiful bawling of hungry cows was heart rending. Farmers were feeding their cattle dry cornstalks, apples, leaves—anything they could find to keep them alive. Temporary relief came from donations of grain from the Midwest, but it never seemed to be enough. A farmer might have to drive more than 100 miles for a truckload of donated hay that would feed his animals for two or three weeks at the most. But the hope of growing any new feed this year was fast dwindling.

Chicken farmers were hit the worst of all. It wasn't simply a matter of no egg production. Thousands of poultry were dying in a single day from the intense heat. The poultry farmer could do little more than stand by and watch, hoping that there would be some relief. But the relief never seemed to come. The heat and drought dragged on and on.

Becky's family was learning a new meaning for the title "Sanctuary Island." The heat wave had, of course, struck the barrier islands just as it had the rest of the South. Its ferocity, however, was tempered by the encircling waters of the ocean and tidal marshes. The ocean breeze was slight and warm, but at least it was moving air. The ocean waves had been flattened to low ripples, but at least they were wet. And one could still see the blue sky. Further inland the sky was hazy and sullen with stagnant air.

Becky and Dani were listless from the heat. It was simply too hot to be outside during the greater part of the day. They didn't even venture out to swim in the ocean after ten in the morning or before five in the afternoon. They would have fried their feet just trying to walk across the sand to get to the water! They spent most of the day indoors, thankful for air conditioning. But for the first time in the many weeks they had spent on the island, they were bored. They were tired of reading; they were fed up with television; they found games monotonous, and they couldn't even get interested in craft activities. To make matters worse, as the long hot days stretched on they began to get irritable with each other. Not even air conditioning could keep tempers from approaching the boiling point!

Now as they sat at the top of the beach stairs watching the fiery ball of sun rise higher in the morning sky, they knew it was time to head back indoors. But the call of the island's wooded trails was too much to resist. They wrapped their beach towels around their shoulders and headed for the little sandy trail that wound through the sea oats and beach grasses to a wooded area north of the house. The trail led to another area of the beach, but small animal trails led off of it into the scrub.

The woods were not thick and heavily shaded here, for it was too close to the salty ocean air. But they did afford some shelter from the intense rays of the sun, and the slight ocean breeze could still be felt, though it was barely enough to rustle the leaves. Grasses grew in patches of filtered sunlight on the ground along the edge of the trail, and the girls were surprised to see that they still had some tender green shoots sprouting near their bases.

The girls came around a bend in the trail and stopped short, startled by the sight just ahead of them. There, not more than 20 feet away, stood a graceful doe and her young spotted fawn. They were grazing on the tender green shoots of grass along the sides of the trail. The little fawn raised its head with a jerk and looked at them with wide, startled eyes. But mother deer gave them little more than a passing glance and then went back to her feeding. Soon the young fawn relaxed its nervous twitching and returned to grazing beside its mother, keeping close to her slender back legs.

The girls were fascinated. The deer on the island were never molested, but they were not tame. They were usually seen only in the early evening and at night, when they grazed on the soft grasses near the island's homes. To see a deer walking nonchalantly through such sparsely sheltering woods in the middle of the day, especially a doe with a young fawn, was rare indeed.

The girls continued to walk slowly up the trail. The lovely animals did not start in fright but moved a few feet into the woods to let them pass. The house was in plain view now. The girls walked backward as they approached it, trying to keep their eyes on the beautiful animals. They climbed the steps to the back porch and turned to look for the deer again. There they were, moving along the edge of the woods close to the lawn.

"It's the heat and drought that's bringing them this close to the house in the middle of the day," said Becky. "They act like nothing really matters to them. Maybe they're as bored as we are and are just trying to stir up a little excitement."

Dani climbed up onto the porch rail, grabbed the supporting post, and sat down, with her legs swinging over the edge. "I think that they're just so hot and hungry that they've forgotten their fear. I bet they're awfully thirsty, too. This drought must be drying up a lot of those little fresh water ponds and lagoons on the island."

"Hey!" exclaimed Becky. For the first time in weeks she was showing a spark of enthusiasm. "I bet you're right. We should go check those places and see what's happening to them. Maybe the deer are being driven out of the deeper woods, looking for water."

An exploratory trip was planned for late that very afternoon. Now that the long summer days stretched the sunlight until nearly nine o'clock in the evening, their outdoor activities could be planned for the cooler evening hours. They spent the day going over the maps they had plotted of the island's waterways. They would make no attempt to go by canoe, for the creek running under the little bridge near the road was too low.

Fortunately, on one of their last exploratory trips to the southwestern portion of the island they had discovered an old trail. They had to do some clearing of brush, but by following it from Otter Slide Pond they found that it brought them out to the central road. They had never seen the pond from the road end before, because it had been blocked by a fallen tree, tall grasses, and a tangle of vines and shrubs. They decided to leave the road entrance camouflaged as they had found it.

By six that evening, the girls had prepared themselves for their new adventure. The preparation process was vital for summer evening trips through the interior. They wore light, comfortable clothing but something that covered their arms and legs sufficiently to avoid the stinging pests that inhabit the interior of the island. They carried bug repellent with them and sprayed it generously on their clothing, as well as on any exposed skin. The spray would not keep ticks or chiggers off. The girls had learned to constantly check their skin and clothing for these minute blood-sucking members of the spider family.

They rode their bikes to within several feet of the trail and hid them behind some bushes. Other than the bug repellent, they carried little more than a canteen and a pair of binoculars. The air felt heavy and fetid as they hiked deeper into the woods. It sapped their strength quickly and brought out beads of perspiration on their faces that would not evaporate, because of the high humidity.

Here in the deep woods, not a breath of air stirred. The humidity clung to them like a winter coat. The woods were perfectly still. Not a bird twittered or a leaf rustled. The thick mat of pine needles that blanketed the trail muffled their footsteps, and if it weren't for the occasional snapping of a dry twig under their feet, they would have questioned their sense of hearing. The utter silence gave the girls a weird feeling—as though time itself hung in suspension.

The sudden loud buzzing sound that seemed to surround them took them completely by surprise. They were being dive-bombed by something large, round, and furry! "Bees!" yelled Dani, swinging the binoculars wildly around to ward off the attack. Her actions only served to intensify the attack. She was sure that an entire swarm of bees were after her; she could feel the sudden sharp burning pain first on her leg and then on her back. Becky had the can of bug repellent and came to Dani's rescue. She was amazed to find that all this fury was coming from only one insect. But what a dynamo of anger he was!

The intrepid explorers decided it was time to retreat. They limped home, with Dani in pain all the way. The stings were turning into large swollen welts. This was obviously not going to be the greatest summer! What had happened to their island paradise?

Later that evening the girls pulled out their field guides to find out the nature of their enemy. He was formidable, indeed! They discovered that they had been rudely introduced to the large miner bees who dig their nests in tunnels in the ground. The book said that these bees could live alone but that they were generally "sociable bees." "Well, he wasn't being very sociable when I met him!" retorted Dani.

It was three days before the swelling on Dani's leg and back had gone down enough, and their courage had built up enough, for the girls to venture out again. This time they both carried bug repellent. Spraying it on their bodies was obviously not sufficient. They would have to spray it on the bees' bodies, too! Fortunately, the ammunition was not needed this time. They reached the lake with no difficulty.

They could smell the lake before they saw it. Now they understood the reason for the fetid air. The repugnant odor of stagnant water lying still too long in the broiling rays of the summer sun assailed their nostrils. The lake water, what little there was of it, looked like some sort of witch's brew. The once muddy and grass-lined banks were dry and cracked; white sedimentary deposits lay in wavy lines, layer upon layer. The stagnant water was thick and dark green with algae. It looked solid enough to walk across!

This was a place of death, and the girls had no desire to stay here. Their hearts sank as they remembered the beauty of the place just last spring. Now they understood the change in the animals. They began to realize what Adam and Eve must have felt when they first saw the effects of sin on their paradise world. As beautiful as this island was, it was just as subject to sin and death as the rest of the world. Their steps were slow and heavy as they headed back to the house.

The question was, what could the girls do to help the

wildlife of the island? They started putting pans of fresh water out around the house each day, but this was hardly sufficient. The family was used to island living and they always brought with them a good supply of fresh water in five-gallon jugs. But they couldn't jeopardize their own water supply; it might have to last quite a while.

Then there was the problem of food. Grasses were drying up and even the greener grasses nearest the beach would soon be overgrazed and dying. There were many young fawns and nursing does in the herds, which needed green grass.

After a few days of deep thought and discussion with Mom and Dad, as well as a few phone calls to local conservation and wildlife authorities, the girls came up with a few possibilities. Most of the residents on the island were animal lovers. The girls would enlist their help, making it a real community effort. If each home would help supply some drinking water, at least some animals could be saved.

The food supply was solved in another way. Becky's mom knew that most large grocery chain stores threw out a considerable supply of old and partially spoiled produce—vegetables and fruits that would not sell to discriminating shoppers. The family made several trips into town to visit the grocery stores, and came back with crates full of corn, lettuce, cucumbers, and all sorts of fruits and other vegetables. A few soft or rotten spots here or there wouldn't bother a hungry deer! Feeding stations were set up near the water supplies. The girls made regular rounds of the stations and found that the food and water were not being wasted.

Despite the rigors of the drought, the excessive heat, the power shortages that occurred almost daily on the island, the smell of stagnant water, and the general boredom of long hours indoors, the girls began to feel a sense of accomplishment. This little sea island had given them so much; now they were able to give something of themselves, to return a small portion to the natural environment of the island.

The drought on the barrier sea islands came to an end with a literal boom. Dark thunder clouds began filling the sky on a humid evening in early August. Thunder rumbled through the sky like the echoing reports of ships' cannon. Becky and Dani stood on the porch deck and watched the approaching storm as it rolled and tumbled its way in from the north. Brilliant bolts of lightning flashed from the ominous black clouds, stabbing at the sea and setting it aboil. Choppy waves came rolling in with ground-shaking force, spewing white foam through the air as they crashed against the seawall.

The storm was upon them before they knew it. The bolt of lightning that sent them diving for the protection of the house was preceded by a sharp snapping in the air around them. The lightning must have hit a nearby transformer, for electric power on the entire island was cut off in that same split second of time. The outside air temperature dropped nearly 20 degrees in less than an hour. Then came the rains! It was as though giant buckets in the sky had been storing all the rain that should have fallen on the island for the past two months. That last great bolt of lightning must have cut through the restraining ropes that held the buckets.

That first storm spent its fury in less than an hour, but others followed in quick succession. Heavy afternoon and evening thunderstorms continued for an entire week. They were storms of renewal, washing stagnation from the islands and leaving them clean and fresh. It was a dramatic version of nature's purging process.

But not quite everything had been purged away. A little something special remained from that time of heat and drought—at least through the last few weeks of summer vacation. It was a bond that still existed between the animals that came to feed and water at the stations, and the two girls who had so faithfully kept watch. For the remainder of that summer a yearling buck, a doe, and a little spotted fawn could often be seen throughout the day, nibbling on the green grasses or resting in the cool shade near the home of their benefactors. It was a parting gift to Becky and Dani, for it would be their last time together on the island.

Chapter 11

A Sanctuary of Memories

The bright rays of the warm southern sun filtered through the spiked palmetto fronds, creating glimmering patches of light on the layers of brown leaves and pine needles that covered the ground. The sun was a warm kiss now, not the searing breath of a blast furnace as it had been a month ago. The island seemed to have forgotten the heat wave and drought. Its recovery had been rapid. That is the way of sea islands—places of sudden change.

The dried-out bracken fern had been replaced by soft green brackets. The rains had washed the island with flowers. White and pink periwinkles bloomed in profusion, and vines of purple morning glory and orange-yellow trumpet flowers climbed their way to the top of palmetto trees, a welcome mat of color that attracted honey bees and hummingbirds. The woods were full of lavender beach peas and delicate yellow wild indigo, and yellow sea oxeye daisies bloomed along the dune lines.

Walks along woodland trails were no longer expeditions into silence. The woods were alive again, filled with the cheery calls of Carolina wrens and the constant buzzing of cicadas. Mockingbirds, the Southland's sweetest singer, flashed through the trees, letting the world know of their joy. But most refreshing of all was the lovely sound of the wind sighing through the tops of pines and live oaks, and setting

the garlands of Spanish moss to swaying.

Becky and Dani were in the perfect place to enjoy not only the sound of the wind but also its reviving coolness. They had hiked nearly three miles through the dense woodland trail, forded the creek, and arrived at Coon Tail Lagoon in the late afternoon of a warm August day.

Now they were perched high in the upper branches of their favorite lookout tree, an old live oak that hung over the banks of the lagoon. From their vantage point they could spot a large alligator sunning itself on the far bank. And on one of the tiny islands in the center stood a graceful white egret, mirrored against the still waters of the lagoon. The alligator slid quietly into the water, but the sharp-eyed egret was quick to detect the reptile's approach. Spreading its great white wings, it lifted into the air, its long neck held in a graceful S curve.

The girls felt something akin to envy for the beautiful bird and its apparent carefree existence on this lovely island. How they would love to spend their days on the banks of this lagoon or soar through the skies above Sanctuary Island!

But their time on the island was coming to a close. The days they had spent here had indeed been some of the most carefree of their lives. But responsibility and change were calling them. Soon each would be going her separate way. The childhood years of grade school were over. Their last summer of total freedom was near its end. September would find each of them in different academies. Dani would be going to a boarding academy some 200 miles from home, while Becky would attend a day academy near her home.

Both girls, in a way, were looking forward to the new experiences. They had applied themselves to their school work and earned good grades. Now the challenge of competition in larger classes and more difficult subject matter began to interest and excite them. They were not really sorry that their lives were changing, but they did have ambivalent feelings when it came to summer vacations and spring breaks.

Next summer both girls would be old enough to find jobs. They wanted the independence that earning their own money would afford them, but that meant that Sanctuary Island would be out of the question. Becky's folks might spend a week or two on the island, but it would never be the same again. No long lazy summers of kite flying, roaming through the marshes and woodlands, or surfing in the ocean waves.

And so the girls spent their last week trying to fit in every activity that they possibly could, as though they were storing up the pleasures of the island for later reference. They knew that the island would still be there, waiting, but they would not. The week was flying by, one day seeming to go faster than the one before.

"Well, Dani," said Becky as she swung down to a lower branch of the old oak, "tomorrow is the last day. What, besides packing, are we going to do?"

"I don't know," replied Dani. "I'd rather not even think about it." The girls sat in moody silence for several long minutes, each lost in her own thoughts. Then, without breaking the silence, they jumped down to the ground and started down the trail for home. They were saying a silent goodbye to the lovely deep woods with its hidden waterways and timid wildlife.

They reached the house just a little before sunset and sat on the porch deck, watching the transformation of the ocean with the changing light of evening. The colors went from a greenish-brown to a gentian blue, flecked with shimmering gold from the last rays of the setting sun. And as the flecks of gold winked out and disappeared, the ocean faded into a liquid black, reflecting, as though from its very depths, brilliant pinpoints of starlight.

Becky was the first to break the silence. "I'm going to be up before the sun tomorrow. I'd like to walk to the northeast beach and watch the sun come up over the ocean. Mom says that we're leaving by ten o'clock and I don't want to miss our last few hours on the island."

The girls were up, dressed, and on their way down the beach by 5:00 a.m. They carried flashlights, for the darkness was intense. They hiked northward along sand that had been packed smooth and firm by the receding waves. The tide had taken the ocean far out, leaving behind wide dunes, flat-domed islands of sand surrounded by sea water. They could hear the waves at a distance, pounding and digging away at the outer dunes, constantly changing the shape of the beach.

Suddenly the beam of their flashlight caught the scudding form of a ghost crab, and they became intently aware of how well it was named. Here in the blackness that fused sand, water, and sky, the tiny creature appeared to be floating, suspended in space like the wraith it was named for. Moving in its odd sideways pattern, the crab scurried out of the beam of light and disappeared, as though it had never been.

The inky blackness of night was giving way to shadowy gray as the girls approached Sand Dollar Beach. They could just make out the broken pilings of the old pier and the driftwood remnants of drowned trees, their smoothed skeletal roots rising from the water. The pilings and trees looked black against the backdrop of the horizon, for a rosy-pink glow was setting the eastern sky on fire. The rays of light shot upward like fiery wings, till the cloud bottoms were burning embers. The scene was breathtaking! The girls sat watching in awed silence.

All of nature came alive! A warm glow touched the faces of the two young girls sitting on the broken seawall. The glow seemed to flow through them, to awaken in them a new feeling. This was not a goodbye to their lovely island sanctuary. It was the beginning! They would see the island again and again. It would be there when they watched a sunrise or smelled the ocean. When they saw the graceful form of a deer or the quizzical face of a raccoon, their minds' eye would carry them back. When the world moved too fast and grew too old, they could walk their imaginations back down its peaceful beaches, or run them swiftly along its wooded trails. Sanctuary Island was theirs forever!